The Great
Hot Sauce Book

The Great
Hot Sauce Book

Jennifer Trainer Thompson

Photographs by Kristen Brochmann

Ten Speed Press
Berkeley, California

Foremost I'd like to thank Phil Wood, who inspired this book. I'm also grateful to Kristen Brochmann for his beautiful photography, my husband Joe for his good design sense and consummate computer skills, my editor Clancy Drake, my publicist Cynthia Traina, and my agent Stuart Krichevsky. Thanks, too, to Lisa Esposito and Jody Fijal for their wizardry and efficiency in the kitchen, to Tim Eidson for his generosity in sharing his knowledge about the hot sauce world, to Larry Joseph and Packaged Facts for making their report on the hot sauce industry available to me, to Andrew Keeler for sharing some of his weirder sauces with me, and to all the lively sauce makers in the business who make this work fun.

Ten Speed Press
P.O. Box 7123
Berkeley, CA 94707

Distributed in Australia by E.J. Dwyer Pty Ltd; in Canada by Publishers Group West; in New Zealand by Tandem Press; in South Africa by Real Books; and in the United Kingdom and Europe by Airlift Books.

Text and cover design by Design Site
Design by Tracy Dean
Illustrations by Jack D. Myers
Photographs by Kristen Brochmann
Printed in Korea by Sung In

Library of Congress Cataloging in Publication Data
Thompson, Jennifer Trainer
    The great hot sauce book / by Jennifer Trainer Thompson : photographs by Kristen Brochmann.
        p.   m.
    Includes index.
    ISBN 0-89815-783-8
    1. Cookery (Hot pepper sauces) 2. Hot pepper sauces. 1.Title.
    TX819.H66T49   1995
    641. 6' 384—dc20   95-34469
                              CIP

1 2 3 4 5 6 7 8 9 10 —99 98 97 96 95

Contents

Introduction

I started collecting hot sauces a few years ago, and couldn't get guests out of my pantry. They'd stand in front of the shelves of bottles and hoot at the names: Last Rites, Pain Is Good, Armageddon, and a hundred others. Then they always wanted to sample them. Their reactions show perfectly why I am so passionate about hot sauce: Because it tastes great, and it makes me laugh.

Three years ago my husband and I created a hot sauce poster—basically a photograph of our pantry shelves—and I remember standing in the printer's office, check in hand, wondering if we had gone mad, or whether anyone else would find the sauces as appealing as we did. Fortunately a lot of people did, and, like my dinner guests, they wanted to know more. In this book I'm able to include information about the sauces (heat levels, types of chiles, flavor, history of the maker) that we couldn't squeeze onto the poster and its sequel.

In the past few years, there's been a general surge of interest in hot sauces. As people look for ways to eliminate salt and butter from their diet without sacrificing flavor, they are discovering that hot sauces—a liquid blend of chile peppers and fruits, vegetables, or herbs—are a marvelous and healthful way to enliven food. Moreover, as we are exposed to increasingly diverse ethnic influences—it is not uncommon to find Thai, Vietnamese, and even Malaysian restaurants now in many cities—people are opening up to foreign flavors and spicy touches.

But passion about hot sauces goes deeper than other food trends. Hot sauce lovers are downright fanatical about the flavors, whose intensity can render you speechless. Anyone who has taken on the habanero knows that flash of pain, followed by a quiet lightheaded euphoria that sends you back for more. And people love the names and labels, whose outrageousness is unparalleled. Can you imagine an olive oil called *Religious Experience*? A bean dip named *Screaming Sphincter*? Even microbrewery beers—with creative, evocative labels—are tame by comparison. Anything goes on hot sauce labels, with imagery ranging from atomic explosions to topless dancers. "How could anyone like a sauce called *Nuclear Waste*?" sniffed one traditional Louisiana sauce maker. But that's part of the

fun—the names make us laugh, and say a lot about what
we're about to experience. This book is a visual as much
as culinary guide to the world of hot sauces.

Hot sauces have been around for centuries—when
Christopher Columbus landed in the Caribbean in the late
1400s, natives were using pepper juices to preserve meats.
Pepper-based sauces are an integral part of Mexican, Asian,
African, and Caribbean cooking. (For more on the culinary
history of hot sauces, see my previous cookbook, *Hot Licks*.)
Americans are perhaps most familiar with Louisiana-style
hot sauces, made with aged cayenne or tabasco peppers,
vinegar, and salt. Indeed, McIlhenny's Tabasco, made by
the same family since the end of the Civil War, accounts
for over 27 percent of the hot sauce market. But there are
many other kinds of hot sauces—made with habaneros,
chipotles, or green jalapeños—and perhaps the strongest
indication of the growing popularity of hot sauces is that,
whereas ten years ago you could find habanero hot sauces
only in the Caribbean and Mexico, today they are every-
where in North America. These boutique sauces now
account for 15 percent of the U.S. market.

Many boutique sauces are made in the United States, borrowing from culinary traditions from around the world. The
story is often familiar: some guy with a passion for peppers
starts making a sauce (often after a youthful trip to a warm
climate), and his friends encourage him to bottle it. He sells
a case to the local grocery store, and he is in business.
Iconoclastic and individualistic, many sauce makers have
full time jobs: by day they are teachers, insurance salesmen,
agricultural researchers, and stockbrokers; by night they are
brewmasters. Many are men (yes, it's a male dominated
business) in their thirties and forties who come from dis-
parate lifestyles and professions, but are linked by a love
of hot food. And they have wonderful stories to tell of the
lengths to which customers go for their sauce: the man who
paid twenty-three dollars for shipping alone to have a bottle
of sauce sent to Japan; the guy who papered his basement
walls with hot sauce labels; or the woman who carries it in
her gym bag for fear of suffering withdrawal.

What's the trend? The hotter the better, but taste counts
too. At hot and spicy food festivals and in cooking classes,
I'm always asked: "What's the hottest sauce on the market?"
A few people are seeking revenge, others like being macho,
while some people just can't seem to get their food hot
enough. Demand for the most incendiary sauce possible

has prompted some makers to market vials of capsaicin (the chemical that gives chiles their sting), which to my mind is akin to extracting caffeine from coffee: caffeine is very powerful (and can kill you), but it misses the point—taste. Sophisticated in their palates, most Americans are looking for heat and flavor—not just burn—and I suspect the most flavorful sauces will be the most enduring. (Incidentally, the heat of a chile is measured in Scoville units, developed by pharmacologist Wilbur Scoville in the early 1900s. Jalapeños, for example, range from 2,500–5,000 Scoville units, while the incendiary habanero weighs in at 150,000–326,000 units.)

A hundred years ago, when the availability of ingredients often defined a hot sauce style, sauces were easily characterized by geography. Today regional distinctions become blurred, as people take their culinary traditions with them to new countries, and fresh exotic produce is available worldwide. This book categorizes sauces geographically when they are made according to a distinct tradition. It also includes a chapter called "The Melting Pot," which covers unusual sauces that borrow from a variety of traditions. And five chapters are dedicated to some crazy corners of the hot sauce world—from the "Politically Incorrects" to the "Untouchables."

A few hot sauce-savoring tips:

There is a huge variety of flavor in hot sauces. Sample them on unsalted tortilla chips or crackers, or simply shake a few drops into the palm of your hand and lick.

Antidotes to heat include milk, yogurt, and other dairy products.

As a general rule, the weirder the bottle, the more interesting the sauce. Odd shaped bottles are an indication that a sauce is made in small batches. Some of the best sauces in the West Indies come in corked beer bottles, recycled juice bottles, or rum flasks.

If a hot sauce has fruit or vegetables in it, refrigerate after opening if you're not going to consume it within the month.

🌶 It's easy to buy fifty sauces in one shop, but that's no fun. The best hot sauces tell a story, taking you back to a city or island you've visited. Hunt for them at airport shops, in restaurants, at corner markets, and in urban ethnic neighborhoods.

🌶 Many collectors buy two sauce bottles: one to keep, and one to trade.

🌶 Host a hot sauce tasting. Set out ten to twenty of your favorite sauces with tortilla ships. People will dive into them, laughing at labels and comparing tastes.

🌶 Anything salt can do, hot sauce can do better. Shake it on pizza, burgers, vinaigrettes, steamed vegetables, salsas, sandwiches, rice and beans, eggs, potato salad, or anything grilled. Tuck it into your bag to improve airline food.

How many hot sauces are there in the world? Tens of thousands. A friend of mine found a tiny warehouse in Auckland, New Zealand, that had over a thousand Chinese hot sauces, none of which he'd seen before. In many Caribbean islands and Mexican villages, there's a bottled hot sauce for every serious cook. Cataloguing them telephone book style would be a fruitless task, because what you list today will be out of date tomorrow. This book is a comprehensive guide to many of the best I've encountered—the most flavorful, the hottest, the wittiest, and the rarest.

Jennifer

🌿 no preservatives

🌶 mild

🌶🌶 spicy

🌶🌶🌶 getting hot

🌶🌶🌶🌶 scorcher

🌶🌶🌶🌶🌶 unbearably hot

SAUCES

Caribbean Sauces

Caribbean sauces are often characterized by the use of habanero or Scotch bonnet peppers (50 to 100 times hotter than jalapeños), which are combined with tropical fruits and vegetables, mustard, and spices. This section includes sauces from the islands of the West Indies and the Caribbean littoral, as well as American-made sauces in the Caribbean tradition.

A Taste of Paradise Caribbean Sunshine

St. John

With fresh herbs and vegetables, this sauce is made in small batches by Cheryl Miller, who gathers the bell peppers, basil, arugula, thyme, chives, and other ingredients from local farmers. Fired with Scotch bonnet, Thai red, and red jalapeño peppers, the sauce is so popular locally that Cheryl has a tiny retail shop in front of her kitchen overlooking Cruz Bay Harbor, which "only the truly inquisitive or tenacious find."

Bandana's XXtra Serious Habanero Pepper Sauce

Pennsylvania

While vacationing in Florida seven years ago, Ted Dames (that's he on the label) got hooked on Melinda's (see page 18). Returning home to "subtropical Pennsylvania," he developed his own sauce, which he tested at a barbecue party that doubled as his wedding reception (brave guy). The party has since mutated into the annual Bandana's Blues BBQ for Hot Food and Cool Jazz, which attracts national performers and is open to the public. Homemade, this herbaceous sauce is filled with fresh onions, garlic, vinegar, and Scotch bonnets countered by a tinge of sweetness from the fresh carrots. Ted also makes a **Serious Habanero Pepper Sauce** ( ) that's sweetened with carrot juice. No salt or sugar.

Baron West Indian Hot Sauce

St. Lucia

A classic West Indian hot sauce developed by a husband-and-wife team on St. Lucia, who blended fresh Scotch bonnet peppers with their home-style island mustard sauce. In the last four years, their cottage operation has mushroomed into a thriving, privately owned company of authentic West Indian food products.

Big John's Famous Key West Hot Sauce

Florida

Intriguingly tart with vinegar and pickled carrots, this sauce is bottled only when Scotch bonnet and local red peppers are in season and can be picked fresh. Conceived as an additive for Bloody Mary's and chili, each bottle is numbered and signed. Big John is a competition cook who takes a lot of second prizes around Key West because "the winners use more of my sauce." He says a lot of Key West expatriates living in Costa Rica create a high demand there for his sauce. He also makes *Big John's Famous Key West Really, Really Hot Sauce* ( ), which is great on conch and fritters.

Blazin' Saddle Habañero Pepper Extra Hot Sauce

Belize

Made with aged habaneros, fresh carrots, onions, lime juice, vinegar, garlic, and salt, this sauce is imported by D.L. Jardine's in Buda, Texas, who gives it a southwestern look and descriptive name—to which those who have been made saddle sore by hot sauce can attest.

Bonney Pepper Sauce

Barbados

Known as bonney peppers in Barbados, Scotch bonnets give this classic mustard-yellow island sauce its heat, which blends nicely with the onions, mustard flour, and turmeric.

Busha Browne's Pukka Hot Pepper Sauce

 Jamaica

Charles Adolphys Thorburn Browne (aka Charlie Browne, pronounced Brow-NE) is a descendent of Peter Howe Browne, Second Marquess of Sligo, an Irishman and governor of Jamaica until 1836, the year slavery was abolished. The "bushas" were nineteenth-century Jamaican planters who, after testing their skills on the polo fields, would throw lavish dinners to determine who could serve the hottest dishes. Having grown up at his ancestral home in western Jamaica, Charlie dug into family archives for nineteenth-century Jamaican sauce recipes, including this seamless one of Scotch bonnet peppers, vinegar, and spices. He's since sold the company to a conglomerate, but the Busha Browne product line is still first rate, and includes *Busha Browne's Spicy & Hot Pepper Sherry Sauce* ( ), a simple blend of sherry and Scotch bonnet peppers.

Busha Browne's Spicy Jerk Sauce

Jamaica

During the days of slavery in Jamaica, runaway slaves survived in the rocky and nearly inaccessible hills of the island by hunting wild animals, especially boar, then "jerking" or curing their meat by rubbing it with spices and slow-cooking it over a fire of pimiento branches. While nothing beats true pit-cooked jerk, you can spice up any barbecue with jerk sauce—basically a hot pepper sauce that's sweetened with sugar, herbs, and spices. This blend includes cane sugar, tomato paste, scallions, thyme, and spices.

Captain Redbeard's Habanero Pepper Sauce

Florida

A smooth kosher blend of habaneros, carrots, onions, vinegar, garlic, lime juice, and salt, developed by a tugboat captain who couldn't stay out of the galley. Liberal amounts of garlic and key limes give this sauce a unique flavor.

Chief Trinidad Hot Sauce

Trinidad

There's nothing fancy about the label, which is a dead giveaway that Chief is intense and authentic, and the sauce of choice in many ethnic markets in the United States. Made in Trinidad since 1957 by a large exporter of spices and condiments, this sauce includes local habaneros, starch, and spices.

Country Home Hot Pepper Sauce

Barbados

A pretty, piercing, yellow mustard-based sauce from Barbados that is flecked with fresh red Scotch bonnet peppers and tempered (barely) by onions and papayas.

Devil Drops

Florida

When customers kept stealing the homemade hot sauce from tables at Barnacle Bill's Seafood House in St. Augustine, Christopher Way started bottling it. Made with the local datil pepper (a close cousin of the habanero, said to have made its way to Florida via indentured servants from Minorca in the 1700s), the sauce is a well-rounded, nicely fruity blend of carrots, passion fruit, mangos, and lime juice. Increased demand led Chris to create a datil farm in St. Augustine, where 2,500 plants are naturally pest patrolled by 10,000 lady bugs. He also makes a milder ***Dat'l-Do-It Hot Sauce*** .

Edun's Caribbean Pepper Sauce

🌶️🌶️🌶️ 🌿   *Puerto Rico*

Moving to Puerto Rico from Guyana, Wendy Lisa Carter couldn't find the hot, rich flavors she and her husband loved, and started making her own hot sauce. (Unlike many islands in the West Indies, Puerto Ricans don't favor hot foods, and their hot sauces tend to be mild.) Sold in small shops and church bazaars around the island, Edun's is a smooth blend of yellow habaneros, mustard, and onions, with spices added pot by pot, by taste, using a great aunt's recipe.

Erica's Country Style Pepper Sauce

🌶️🌶️🌶️🌶️   *St. Vincent*

From an island in the lower Caribbean that struggles with economic development, this sauce is made by an all-Vincentian-owned company, using locally grown peppers from Kingstown. It's a simple, coarse sauce, with habaneros, salt, and water.

Evadney's Fire Water Habanero Hot Table Sauce

🌶️🌶️🌶️ 🌿   *California*

A thin blend of vinegar, Jamaican habaneros, onions, ginger, honey, herbs, and spices, made by a transplanted Jamaican living in Los Angeles.

Evadney's All-Purpose Jamaican Hot Sauce

🌶🌶🌶   *California*

A thick, spicy, slightly sweet mahogany-colored sauce with habaneros, onions, garlic, ginger, allspice, ketchup, and a hint of cinnamon. The recipe is from a family housekeeper in Jamaica named Evadney, who has since moved back to the mountains to join her family and other members of the Maroons tribe (formerly runaway Jamaican slaves who perfected the art of jerked foods).

Eve's Pepper Sauce

🌶🌶🌶🌶   *Tobago*

Sometimes the simplest sauces are the best, such as this bright, fresh one from Tobago, sold in local stalls at farmers' markets.

Forbes Ground Red Peppers

🌶🌶🌶🌶   *Costa Rica*

A scorching sauce found in an ethnic grocery store in Brooklyn, made with habaneros, vinegar, and salt. Direct and no frills.

Grand Anse Moko Jumbie Grill Sauce

St. Thomas

During carnival, storytellers dressed as spirits (moko jumbies) used to walk on stilts from village to village, often accompanied by fief bands, telling stories and gossiping about the townspeople. Originally from Grenada, the sauce is now made by Calypso Limited in St. Thomas, and is a mild but spirited blend of Scotch bonnets, mangos, onions, ginger, and cinnamon, with a strong whiff of clove. They also make *Grand Anse Peppa-Po* ( ), *Island Jerk*, ( ) and *Moki Moki Mustard Sauce* ( ).

Gray's Hot Pepper Sauce

Jamaica

Thin as a Louisiana sauce and just as salty, this fiery sauce of habaneros, vinegar, sugar, and salt has been made in Jamaica for over thirty years by the Gray family.

Grenfruit Hot Sauce

Grenada

This punchy Scotch bonnet sauce is distinguished by its use of pawpaw (green papaya) and condicion, a small, cucumberlike vegetable grown on Grenada that provides an acidic base. The sauce is made by the Grenfruit Women's Cooperative, a work program in rural Grenada established by the Catholic church to provide training and employment to women of the area, especially high school dropouts. Founded in the late 1970s, the co-op has expanded from its original line of candied fruits to include ground, packaged spices and, since 1986, hot sauces. *Grenfruit Spicy Sauce* ( ) is a milder but full-bodied sauce from a rural women's work cooperative in Grenada, packed with green mangos and onions, and fragrant with ginger, cinnamon, and especially clove.

Gunsam's Hot Sauce

St. Vincent

A traditional Caribbean sauce in a ketchup bottle, from the Grenadines, with local hot peppers, pawpaw (green papaya), garlic, and a light touch of mustard.

Habanero !HOT! !HOT! !HOT! Pepper Sauce

Colorado

A Panamanian-style habanero sauce, with onions, vinegar, and plenty of prepared mustard, made by Alois Dogue, a Panamanian who moved to Colorado twenty-three years ago.

Heatwave North Side Hot Sauce

St. Thomas

Sweet with fresh papaya, fired up with Scotch bonnets, and made interesting with numerous herbs that float through this spicy sauce, Heatwave was developed in a restaurant kitchen where Terry O'Hara worked. For a long time, Terry hand colored the black-and-white labels late at night after working two jobs. The first case, which was given on consignment to a shop in St. Thomas, sold within two weeks, and a company was born. Terry also makes **Heatwave Mango Hot Sauce** ( ).

Hecho En Casa Pique Criollo

Puerto Rico

In Puerto Rico, where you won't often find the super-hot blended habanero sauces common to other Caribbean islands, hot sauces of whole chiles steeping in vinegar (called piques) are common. From the mountains of Cayey, this lovely pique is made with jalapeños, local peppers (ajíes puertorriqueños), cilantro, and other herbs. When the vinegar gets low, natives just add more, and sometimes a little rum or pineapple juice, too.

Hot Licks

Massachusetts

Some hot sauce makers create mini sauces to give away. They are perfect for tucking into your bag (especially on airplane flights), and a popular collector's item to track the evolution of a particular product's label design. I bottled this papaya-based habanero sauce in tiny vials when my hot sauce cookbook, *Hot Licks*, was published in 1994. Six hundred bottles were made, with the label featuring the cover of the book.

Inner Beauty Hot Sauce

Massachusetts

When Chris Schlesinger started bottling this sauce in his Cambridge restaurant, it had a hilarious label, great heat, and tiers of ripe, bold flavor that combined habaneros with mustard, fruit juices, and spices. The sauce became one of Bonnie Raitt's favorites, and general demand led Schlesinger to bottle it in Costa Rica. In 1993, Inner Beauty was picked up by megadistributor Gourmet America and the label was changed (the one shown here is the original), the bottle went from hip-pocket flask to a hunched-shoulder mold, and—distressing to many I.B. fans—the new sauce, which is now bottled in Vermont, is not quite so hot. The flavor is still wonderful, however, and Chris recently commissioned a California grower to develop a hotter and more intensely flavored strain of habanero exclusively for Inner Beauty.

Inner Beauty Real Hot Sauce

               Massachusetts

A dense, stylish sauce with the same ingredients as Inner Beauty Hot Sauce (above), although slightly hotter and not as fruity. (Shown is the new label and bottle.)

Isla Vieques Caribbean 3-Pepper Hot Sauce

Vieques

On a small island off Puerto Rico, Jim and Diana Starke make an extraordinary line of hot sauces that use indigenous herbs, peppers, and fruits. They bottle most of their sauces in rum flasks, taking a tip from locals who use rum bottles of all sizes to "put up" homemade hot sauces. Locals now drop off empty Paulo Viejo bottles in the Starke's driveway, and in three years they've recycled over 80,000 bottles. A triad of cayenne, jalapeño, and habanero chiles in a chunky papaya base gives this sauce a sugar-free sweetness. Other sauces not shown include *Isla Vieques Caribe Fire* ( ), with papayas and habaneros, *Sweet Revenge* ( ), with habaneros, carrot, and tamarind, *Sweet & Spicy Pepper Sauce* ( ), and *Salsa Picante* ( ). They also make a *Hot N' Honey Sauce* ( ), with cayenne chiles, local ajíes puertorriqueños, and honey from Vieques. Originally conceived of as a way to combine Vieques' own bee farm honey with surplus ripe chiles, it's become a favorite among customers, who put it on everything from burritos to ice cream.

Isla Vieques Mountain Herb Hot Sauce

Vieques

Wanting to create a flavor that was indigenous to the island, the Starkes began cooking with recao, a long-leafed coriander that proliferates in Puerto Rico and gives characteristic flavor to many Puerto Rican dishes. This unique herbaceous sauce is thick with papayas, onions, and habaneros, and pungent with recao.

Isla Vieques Pique Puertorriqueño

Vieques

Puerto Ricans love pique, an unblended sauce where chiles and herbs float in vinegar. In native restaurants you'll find piques in used soda bottles, beer bottles, even orange juice bottles. This pretty pique is made with whole chiles, onions, garlic, herbs, and spices.

Island Heat Scotch Bonnet Pepper Sauce

Costa Rica

As a child, Helen Willinsky would slow-cook jerked foods before going off to school in Kingston, Jamaica. She was later educated in Europe, then worked in restaurant kitchens in Switzerland, but returned to her native Jamaican food when establishing her own line of food products, called Helen's Tropical Exotics. She makes authentic jerk seasoning, as well as this Jamaican-style hot sauce, which is slightly fruity from the passion fruit and papayas, but with good heat from the Scotch bonnets.

Island Style Jamaican

🌶️🌶️🌶️   *Jamaica*

A pretty, yellow Caribbean sauce of Scotch bonnet peppers, vinegar, salt, and spices.

Island Treasure Jamaica Wildfire

🌶️🌶️🌶️ 🌿   *Jamaica*

From Jamaica, a clean-tasting sauce with habaneros, water, vinegar, and spices. Their **Island Treasure Papaya Pepper Sauce** (🌶️🌶️🌶️)has a generous streak of papayas, habaneros, vinegar, mustard, and spices.

Jamaica Hell Fire Doc's Special

🌶️🌶️🌶️🌶️   *Florida*

This sauce was developed in the Blue Mountains of Jamaica in the early 1970s by a transplanted German chemist named Dr. Ingolf Duphorn, who searched for the hottest Scotch bonnet peppers he could find in Jamaica and concocted this vibrant sauce using vinegar, salt, and fresh Blue Mountain pimiento (allspice). The sauce is now made in Tampa by folks dedicated to using his original recipe and Jamaican ingredients, including Blue Mountain pimiento. It's a hot one.

Jo B's Chilipaya Island Rojo Sauce

 *Vermont*

Vermont is heating up the hot sauce scene (sounds odd, but true), especially with this Caribbean-style sauce of fresh red habaneros, fresh papayas, cider vinegar, lime juice, and coconut milk. Maker Jo Jenkins took inspiration from some Antiguan co-workers in creating this kicker of a sauce, which is made fresh in small quantities.

Jo B's Gorda'sala Habanero Sauce

Vermont

Gorda'sala is a fusion of Caribbean, Spanish, French, and East Indian cuisines, taught to Jo Jenkins by a woman she worked with in the islands. In addition to the rum, ingredients include habaneros, mustard, papayas, lime juice, onions, coconut milk, garlic, and ginger.

Jump Up and Kiss Me Hot Sauce with Passion

Massachusetts

Logging 6,000 sea miles in sailboat deliveries from New England to the West Indies, I fell in love with Caribbean sauces, and wanted to create one that was fresh, slightly fruity, and packed with tropical flavor. Salt-free, Jump Up and Kiss Me Hot Sauce with Passion has a sweet heat, from blending habaneros, papayas, onions, honey, ginger, garlic, mustard, and spices. I also wanted a non-macho name that evoked the humor and life-loving spirit found in the culture of hot. Not shown are ***Jump Up and Kiss Me Spicy Passion Fruit Sauce*** (   ), made with passion fruit, pineapple, and habaneros, and ***Jump Up and Kiss Me Smoky Chipotle Sauce*** (   ).

Key West's Island Pepper Sauce

Florida

A sweet, dark brown sauce in the Pickapeppa tradition (see page 22), with raisins, mangos, tomato paste, brown sugar, herbs, and a hint of peppers (habanero and jalapeño).

Key West's S.O.B. Jamaican Hot Sauce

Florida

Southern Florida is home to many entrepreneurial hot sauce makers who are putting out high-quality sauces. No matter where it's brewed, a Caribbean-style sauce is obvious from the first whiff, when the fresh floral habanero captures your attention. With a neon pink label, this Jamaican-style hot sauce has habaneros, three tropical fruits (papaya, mango, and tamarind), vinegar, lime juice, and spices.

Lottie's Bajan-Cajun Premium Hot Pepper Sauce

Barbados

Interestingly, the label places this sauce in the Louisiana tradition, though its mixture of red Scotch bonnets, vinegar, salt, onions, and garlic reveals a Caribbean influence. As hot as the Barbados sun.

Lottie's True Bajan Premium Hot Pepper Sauce

🌶️🌶️🌶️🌶️ 🌿   *Barbados*

With a plastic bottle and simple labeling, this Barbadian mustard-based hot sauce is made with yellow Scotch bonnets, vinegar, onions, garlic, sugar, and salt on a colonial plantation that I'm told looks like a scene from *Gone with the Wind*.

Marie Sharp's Habanero Pepper Sauce

🌶️🌶️🌶️🌶️ 🌿   *Belize*

For years I heard about a Belizean woman named Marie Sharp, and how she created the original Melinda's Hot Sauce of legend (named after a town in Belize—see page 18), but that she no longer makes Melinda's (which some aficionados claim has gone downhill as a result). Well, Marie's back (claiming she never left), and has been making hot sauce since 1983 in the Mayan Mountain foothills. She began by peddling her sauce door to door, and says that no one ("except possibly my competition") has tried her sauce and not become a customer. Floral and bracing, Marie Sharp's sauce comes in several heat levels, made with red habaneros, fresh carrots, onions, key lime juice, vinegar, garlic, and salt. I found the taste flavorful and similar to Melinda's Hot Sauce (which has the same ingredients), but perhaps slightly less salty and more habanero flavored.

Marinda's West Indian Hot Sauce

🌶️🌶️🌶️🌶️   *St. Vincent*

A thick, fiery sauce from the lower Caribbean that is still rare in the United States, with habaneros, onions, garlic, vinegar, mustard, and salt.

Matouk's Hot Sauce

Trinidad

Hot, pungent, and as thick as marmalade, Matouk sauces come in ketchup bottles. The Matouk family has been involved in the commercial life of Trinidad and Tobago since 1925; they started a condiment company in 1968 after this former British colony attained its independence. This amber-colored sauce combines red and yellow habaneros with papaya, onions, and mustard. They also make a delicious **MP Flambeau Sauce** ( ) a concentrate of red habaneros, a **Hot Pepper Sauce** ( ) with yellow and red habaneros, and a **Calypso Sauce** ( ) with mustard and yellow habaneros.

Melinda's Hot Sauce

Costa Rica

Manufactured by brothers David and Greg Figuerora of New Orleans, Melinda's Hot Sauce—which the makers say is the original recipe formulated in Belize, but which some assert is the Atlantis of the hot sauce world since production was moved to Costa Rica—has a tasty red habanero base that is subtly flavored with lime juice, onions, and a bit of ground carrot. (Other ingredients include vinegar, garlic, and salt.) They also make **Melinda's Extra Hot Sauce** ( ), **Melinda's XXXtra Hot Sauce** ( ), and **Melinda's XXXXtra Reserve** ( ), all of which contain the same ingredients as Melinda's Hot Sauce, although the two hotter ones are slightly saltier. Not too many years ago, Melinda's was considered one of the hottest sauces on the market, but with the advent of the Untouchables (see page 114), those days are over, and their XXXXtra Reserve is an attempt to keep up with the competition. Each bottle is date-stamped and available in "limited" quantities (only 5,000 cases a year), blended with red habaneros (considered to be sweeter and hotter than other colored habaneros) that are aged for a year to increase their heat. It's versatile and tasty, with a heat level similar to many scorching Caribbean sauces. Melinda's also makes a mild **Amarillo Hot Mustard Pepper Sauce** ( ) with onions, habaneros, sugar, mustard, vinegar, and turmeric.

Miss Anna's Hot Pepper Sauce

🌶️🌶️🌶️🌶️ 🌿   *St. Croix*

I love the label—"the Appetite Food"—of this sauce found in the Virgin Islands. With Scotch bonnets, vinegar, mustard, onions, garlic, curry, and salt, it's made by Rosalie Denis, a St. Lucia native who descends from a long line of St. Lucia fishermen. Her grandfather developed the sauce to eat with his usual meal of fish, and it was handed down to her mother and then to her. "Since marketing [with a] professional-looking bottle," she wrote proudly, "our sales have become international," with fan letters from satisfied customers coming from as far away as the United States.

Miss V's Caribbean Hot Sauce

🌶️🌶️🌶️🌶️ 🌿   *St. Croix*

This fiery sauce of just Scotch bonnets, onions, mustard, salt, and spices has been made since 1981 and packaged since 1994.

Mrs. Tull's Home Made Hot Sauce

🌶️🌶️🌶️🌶️ 🌿   *St. Thomas*

Mrs. Tull's is the kind of sauce I hunt for—clearly homemade (with its pinking-shear label and recycled juice bottle), and bold with vegetables I've never heard of (strongback root, sive onions). Every time I've stumbled upon her sauce, everything about it has changed, including the label, bottle, and flavor (the sauce originally came in a beer bottle with a cork top)—but no matter, they are all rich with huge taste. I wrote to Mrs. Tull, and received a kind letter back from a woman who holds her ingredients close to her vest (clearly she has no intention of conforming to USDA laws), writing that if she told me her ingredients, she would have to give them to the "thousands of people who ask for them over the years." This sauce has a sweet, jerklike heat, with papayas, ginger, garlic, mustard seeds, fenugreek, and habaneros, plus those strongback roots.

Nel's Old Time Scotch Bonnet Hot Sauce

Jamaica

Thick as ketchup, this Scotch bonnet sauce is balanced with papayas, vinegar, and spices. It's made by Tijule, a Jamaican company that packages other native products such as nutmeg jams, lime marmalade, and canned ackee. Tijule also make **Nel's Old Time Hot Curry Sauce** ( ), which is made by adding curry to the Scotch Bonnet Hot Sauce; and **Nel's Old Time Jerk Sauce** ( ), a mild, smooth jerk sauce with scallions, Scotch bonnets, thyme, salt, spices, fruits, and vegetables.

911 Hot Sauce

Illinois

In the flash before the heat of the yellow Jamaican Scotch bonnet explodes in your mouth, there's a faint sweetness of mango (which has a nice mellowing effect on the vinegar), onion, mustard, and many spices. Born in Java, Jan Van Blommesteyn moved to the states as a kid, then spent a few years delivering sailboats to the Caribbean. In an effort to make fresh fish more interesting while at sea, he discovered the Scotch bonnet. Popping one into his mouth, "my respect for the yellow Scotch bonnet pepper was instant, as was my love for the taste."

Outerbridge's Original Sherry Peppers Sauce

Bermuda

The Outerbridges are a ninth-generation Bermuda ship-building family who for the past thirty-five years have been making a sherry pepper sauce that's been a tradition in Bermuda since the late 1800s, when Royal sailors fortified their sherry with chiles to make a seasoning for soups and stews. This tasty family recipe calls for steeping bud Chinese peppers and eighteen herbs and spices in casks of sherry. Try it in rum drinks or martinis.

Outerbridge's Original Devilishly Hot Sherry Peppers Sauce

 Bermuda

Similar to Outerbridge's Original Sherry Peppers Sauce, but hotter. They also make **Outerbridge's Original Sherry Rum Peppers Sauce** ( ), made with rum. (They are all delicious sprinkled on fish chowder, vegetable tarts, or quiche.)

Papa Joe Scotch Bonnet Red Pepper Sauce

Costa Rica

Hard to find anymore in the United States, this sauce is still being made in Costa Rica, and is thinner and more blended than many Caribbean sauces, with red Scotch bonnet peppers, carrots, molasses, and rum.

Pearl's Hot Pepper Sauce

St. Vincent

This fresh, fragrant Vincentian sauce is bright red, nicely garlicked, and studded with habanero seeds.

Pick-a-Pepper Pepper Sauce

Trinidad

This down-island sauce is hot with habaneros, yellow with mustard and egg yolks, and uniquely flavored with a hint of pumpkin.

Pickapeppa Pepper Sauce

Jamaica

With a recipe dating back to 1920, this sauce with its elegant label has been exported from Jamaica for over fifty years. Aged in oak barrels for a year, the sauce is sweet and thick with mangos, raisins, tamarind, tomatoes, and onions, with just a hint of hot peppers. A great cooking sauce or all-around mild table condiment.

Pirates Blend
Caribbean Condiment

Costa Rica

This spicy sauce hasn't much heat from its cayenne peppers, but has loads of flavor from the ginger, mustard, onions, and spices that suggest a hint of curry. It's imported and labeled by Half Moon Bay Trading Company of Florida, which was founded by friends in the advertising and package design business. The recipe was developed by one of the partners, who spent a lot of time in Costa Rica surfing and windsurfing.

Rass Mon

North Carolina

Friends brought Scotch bonnet seeds back from Jamaica in 1970, and the sauce that the Clevenger family made from these early plants was named after a Jamaican friend, whose favorite expression was, "You bet yo' rass, mon!" This sweet sauce is laced with raisins, honey, and allspice. Other ingredients include Scotch bonnet peppers, lime juice, and soy sauce.

Rebel Fire No. 3

🌶️ 🌶️ 🌶️ 🌿   *Ontario*

This heady Jamaican-style sauce is sweet with mangos, hot with Scotch bonnets, and incredibly flavorful with cucumbers, fresh garlic, yellow mustard seed, and masala spices that are freshly ground (including coriander, cumin, turmeric, cardamom, fenugreek, clove, and cinnamon). The sauce began with Guy Allen, who moved to Toronto in the 1960s and missed the hot food of his Arkansas boyhood. He began making pepper sauces to introduce Canadian friends to "capsicum cuisine," and in 1980 met Gaynor Carney, a pepper fanatic from Wales. Together they searched for premium peppers from Africa, the Caribbean, India, and the Southwest, explaining matter-of-factly, "Why go to the trouble of bringing the world's finest chiles up to this northern land unless we could make better sauces than anyone we knew?" Indeed. Made since 1985, their sauces have no salt, sugar, or additives, and are fantastic.

Rica Red Habanero
Banana Jama Sauce

🌶️   *Costa Rica*

Belize born and New Orleans raised, photographer Stuart Jeffrey first encountered the habanero while traveling with his father through Mexico to Belize in 1980. His father told stories about the King of Peppers, and he enjoyed its floral heat in salsas at cantinas along the way. Back in New Orleans, he started making hot sauce, but found chiles in short supply. While photographing the 1984 World's Fair, he met Caribbean heads of state and discussed where he could cultivate the habanero. After visiting growers in eight countries, he decided upon Costa Rica, which isn't exactly known for its spicy foods and hence didn't have big chile harvests (the largest farm was 10 acres!), but on one farm Stuart saw something that caught his attention: a mutant 7-foot habanero plant.

Opening a habanero-testing farm there in 1986, Stuart spent six years developing a hybrid red habanero, which he feels has a unique flavor and short-lived heat that ascends to the back of the mouth. He coined it the Rica Red habanero, and Stuart's Quetzal Foods International (pronounced KET-SAUL) now has the largest habanero farm in the world (he even grows tabascos for McIlhenny), exporting 8 million pounds of peppers yearly. Sweetened with brown sugar and fruit, Banana Jama is a mild habanero sauce with a strong banana flavor and hints of tomato paste and tamarind.

Rica Red Habanero Hot Pepper Sauce

Costa Rica

The salty taste and habanero heat are complemented by carrots, papayas, onions, and lemon juice. Quetzal Foods also makes **Rica Red Habanero Calypso Sun Sauce** (🌶🌶), a full-bodied sauce with Rica Red habaneros, cucumbers, papayas, and onions, and a hint of mustard, and **Rica Red Habanero Maya Moon Sauce** (🌶🌶), a mustard-based sauce with peppers and Rica Red habaneros.

Salu's Jerk Sauce

Jamaica

Spicy but not hot, this thick, dark sauce is flavored with scallions, thyme, habaneros, spices, and caramel food starch.

Salu's Scotch Bonnet Pepper Sauce

Jamaica

Pumpkin orange and thick as ketchup, this Jamaican sauce is scalding with Scotch bonnets, vinegar, mustard, and salt.

Santa Maria Hot Chili Habanero Sauce

Sweden

This Swedish sauce in the Caribbean tradition not only has habaneros and mangos, but also apple juice.

Scott's Jerk Sauce

Jamaica

Almost black and thinner than most jerk sauces, this fragrant sauce is slightly tart and laced with thyme. Other ingredients include scallions, habaneros, vinegar, tomato paste, spices, salt, and sugar.

Sontava! The Original Habanero Pepper Hot Sauce

Belize

This hot, fresh-tasting sauce is similar in flavor to Marie Sharp's sauce (see page 17), with the same ingredients, including red habaneros, carrots, onions, locally grown key limes, vinegar, garlic, and salt. Imported by D.L. Jardine's of Texas.

Spicy Caribee Tangy Pineapple Sauce

Puerto Rico

Bottled by the owner of a quaint shop in Old San Juan, this sauce is a seamless blend of pineapple and local peppers, ajíes puertorriqueños. The inclusion of pineapple is typically Puerto Rican.

The Great Hot Sauce Book

Spitfire Red Hot Pepper Sauce

Barbados

Growing up in Georgetown (his mother was a director of CARE), Leander Hamilton had the early distinction of serving canapes to JFK at his mother's cocktail parties. With her he visited developing nations, tasting his first Bajan pepper sauce with flying fish, christophene, and rice at the age of ten. When his mother moved to Barbados in 1970, he wrote his graduate school thesis on an imaginary company that imported hot sauces. Several years later he decided to go into the business, and has many stories that are typical of sauce entrepreneurs—like the time American Air Cargo lost 100 gallons of his sauce, or the printer ran the first batch of 25,000 labels with "Antilleo" instead of "Antilles" Foods. ("And so Antilleo Foods was born," Leander explained cheerfully.) Now in San Francisco, Leander imports two fragrant, generous sauces made with Scotch bonnets, vinegar, salt, onions, and garlic. They are consummately blended, with a strong heat and fresh finish. Not shown is **Spitfire Hot Pepper Sauce** ( ), which is similar to Spitfire Red Hot Pepper Sauce, but with the addition of mustard and sugar.

Sunny Caribbee Hot Sauce

Tortola

Originally from Maine, the Gunter family moved to Tortola in 1979 and, determined not to sit on the beach drinking rum, looked for a plan. Desiring to foster the production of indigenous food and crafts, they opened the Sunny Caribbee gift shop in a cottage near the docks in Tortola in 1983, selling island seasonings and condiments under their own label. This sauce is made with habanero and bird peppers, vinegar, water, spices, and mustard.

Sunny Caribbee XXX Calypso Hot

Tortola

Sunny Caribbee's hottest sauce, with red habaneros, vinegar, water, and spices.

Susie's Original Hot Sauce

🌶️🌶️🌶️🌿   *Antigua*

Susannah Tongue's mother, Rosemarie, ran a boarding house in Antigua, cooking for the Royal Antigua police force, school kids, and other guests who loved her spicy foods. Her pepper sauce was renowned, and when asked how she learned to make it, Rosemarie would claim, "It was a vision from God." Susannah still remembers the shed out back with the grinding table for peppers, where the kids pitched in. Susannah is carrying on the tradition with her mother's recipe, which blends Scotch bonnets, West Indian red, and habanero peppers with mustard, vinegar, and spices in a voluptuous heat.

Tamarindo Bay Pepper Sauce

🌶️   *Costa Rica*

From Half Moon Bay Trading Company, this mild sauce is fragrant with banana, pineapple, and tamarind, and sweetened with molasses. It's a good marinade for chops, cut with 50 percent beer and loads of garlic. *Tamarindo* is not only Spanish for tamarind, but is also a small village on the northern Pacific coast of Costa Rica where the surfing is awesome.

Tipica Jalapeño Sauce

🌶️🌶️   *Costa Rica*

Imported and labeled by Lousiana-based Quetzal Foods (see page 23), this tart, green jalapeño sauce has sweet peppers, white vinegar, and spices mild enough for the vegetable quality of the jalapeños to shine through. They also make **Tipica Passion Fruit Hot Sauce** (🌶️🌶️), which combines passion fruit with papayas, cucumbers, onions, habaneros, mustard seed, and spices for a mild, fruity flavor; **Tipica Pineapple Hot Sauce** (🌶️), a mild, dark sauce emphasizing the tamarind and pineapple, complemented by a hint of habaneros, spices, and caramel; and **Tipica Tamarind Hot Sauce** (🌶️), which is similar to Tipica Pineapple Sauce, but with bananas.

Trader Rick Bonny Pepper Island Hot Sauce

🌶🌶🌶   *Barbados*

Georgian Rick Engel (aka Trader Rick) imports and labels these sauces from L.G. Miller & Sons in Barbados, where sauces have been made for three generations. This simple sauce has bonney peppers (sweet, fiery Scotch bonnets grown on Barbardos), onions, garlic, vinegar, and salt. His **Mango/Tamarind Hot Sauce & Marinate** (🌶🌶) combines molasses with mangos, tamarind, tomatoes, and bonney peppers, in a spicy, somewhat salty sauce, and **Mustard/Pepper Bajan Hot Sauce** (🌶🌶🌶), which is a mustard-based sauce with bonney peppers, onions, vinegar, and spices.

Trinidad Mild Habañero Pepper Sauce

🌶🌶   *Florida*

Thirty years ago, Marie Permenter met a Trinidadian seeking investors in a gold mine (seriously). She went down to investigate, fell in love with the island, and sup-ported his venture. Next she was asked to finance a ship-wreck expedition—the boat wasn't worth much, but the propellers were solid brass. By now Mrs. Permenter and the Trinidadian were friends, and when he asked her about bottling his family sauce recipe, she said yes. Mrs. Permenter has since moved to Trinidad, and her children bottle the sauce in Florida. Fresh and herbal, Trinidad sauces come in several heat levels, and are distinguished by the use of celery and green peppers, as well as Spanish thyme, French thyme, sweet basil, and other herbs grown on a mountain range in Trinidad. They use a red Trinidad congo pepper (a large strain of the habanero). Not shown are their **Trinidad Hot Habañero Pepper Sauce** (🌶🌶🌶) and **Trinidad Extra Hot Habañero Pepper Sauce** (🌶🌶🌶).

Trinidad Tropical Marinade & Grilling Sauce

🌶🌶   *Florida*

Hot sauces straight up make ideal grilling marinades, as is evident in this aromatic sauce with habaneros, orange juice, lime juice, onions, garlic, and cilantro. Full flavored and flecked with herbs, it's not as sweet as jerk sauces, and versatile on vegetables, meats, or pizza.

Triple Barn Burner Super Hot Sauce

                               Canada

This fiery sauce is made by a Guyanan who works in food science at the University of Alberta and wanted to bring the flavor of the West Indies to Canada. He first sold his sauce at farmers' markets outside Edmonton, and people kept asking for it hotter, which he obliged with this sauce of habaneros, vinegar, onions, thyme, garlic, spices, and a hint of mustard.

Tropical Tastes Extra Hot Sauce

Belize

Liz Pingel had a restaurant in Nevis, where she experimented with various sauces. She's since moved to Florida, and has this sauce made for her in Belize. With red habaneros, fresh carrots, lime juice, onions, vinegar, garlic, and salt, it's similar in taste to Marie Sharp's sauce (see page 17).

Turban Salsa Picante

Trinidad

Stabbing heat from Trinidad habaneros, with a little garlic, onions, water, and mustard thrown in.

Uncle Billy's Voo Doo Jerk Slather

Maine

Hotter than some jerk sauces, this Caribbean-inspired spicy sauce from Maine has Scotch bonnet peppers, Spanish onions, tamarind, Barbados molasses, honey, mustard, and spices. Try some with fritters and fresh lime, or mix it into ground beef for wonderful hamburgers.

Uncle Willie's Hibiscus Vinegar

St. Thomas

This lovely vinegar has the scent of oregano and taste of French thyme, and takes on a pretty pink color from the hibiscus flowers. It's made with Scotch bonnet peppers, island celery (he claims there's a difference), herbs from Willie's garden, lemon grass, and a touch of Virgin Island rum. Willie suggests adding more white vinegar when the bottle's half full, and using it with everything from steamed vegetables to vinaigrettes.

Uncle Willie's Jammin' Hot Sauce

St. Thomas

Flecked with seeds and thicker than his other sauces, the taste of tomatoes is prevalent in this sauce, complemented by Scotch bonnet peppers and crushed red peppers, cucumbers, molasses, and Virgin Island rum. Willie spent twenty years in restaurant service, but "nothing in my background prepared me for mass production," especially since he plants his own peppers and makes the sauce from scratch. After chopping chiles until 3 A.M. one night, he found himself in his car, cooling his fingers in the air-conditioning vents. The sauce comes in three heat levels.

Uncle Willie's Mangos Jammin' Hot Sauce

🌶🌶🌶

St. Thomas

With more flavor than heat, this sauce is imbued with mangos, Scotch bonnets, vinegar, corn syrup, and rum. Note how Willie cleverly avoids label costs by labeling every bottle the same, and differentiating his sauces by the cap decoration. He also makes **Uncle Willie's Heated Passion Jammin' Sauce** (🌶🌶🌶), which is a light, lovely sauce with passion fruit, Scotch bonnet peppers, vinegar, grenadine, and rum.

Uno Hot Sauce

🌶🌶🌶 🌿

Belize

Victor Medore was introduced to this hot sauce on a Belize fishing trip. Bright orange and light tasting, the red habaneros are complemented by sweet carrots and lime juice. Back in New Jersey, Medore planted habanero seeds and tried to make a similar sauce, but he couldn't get the same heat as with habaneros grown in the Caribbean littoral. The sauce is now bottled in Estan Creek, and Medore says it's Marie Sharp's original recipe (see page 17). Available in two heat levels (not shown is **Uno XXX Hot**, 🌶🌶🌶🌶), denoted by the neck band.

Virgin Fire Dragon's Breath

🌶🌶🌶🌶 🌿

St. John

Bob Kennedy moved to the islands nineteen years ago after it rained sixty-three days in upstate New York. In his bright, relishlike sauces he uses only fresh peppers, which he processes and bottles immediately (rather than preserving them in a vinegar/salt brine), giving his sauces a fresh flavor and aroma. Dragon's Breath is made with habanero peppers, vinegar, lime juice, and salt. Bob also makes **Virgin Fire Pineapple Sizzle** (🌶), **Eastern Caribbean Hot Pepper Sauce** (🌶🌶🌶), **Hot Sweet Ting** (🌶🌶, with ripe jalapeños and cubanelle chiles), and **Papaya Fire** (🌶🌶).

Walker's Wood Scotch Bonnet Pepper Sauce

🌶️🌶️🌶️🌶️   *Jamaica*

With a singular heat and taste, made with Jamaican Scotch bonnets, this sauce is called "hot flash" by the locals because of the pleasing heat and unforgettable impression. Other ingredients include scallions, vinegar, thyme, onions, salt, sugar, and garlic. Marketed from an office in Miami, Walker's Wood sauces are made in Walkerswood, Jamaica; production began in the 1970s to provide work for the villagers there. (Note: On the label is a man who expresses my sentiments exactly on tasting this sauce.)

Walker's Wood Jerk Seasoning

🌶️🌶️🌶️🌶️   *Jamaica*

This jerk sauce is as thick as relish, and fiery with Scotch bonnets, scallions, spices, and a lot of salt.

Walker's Wood Jonkanoo Pepper Sauce

🌶️🌶️🌶️🌶️   *Jamaica*

At Christmastime, Jamaicans celebrate their diverse heritage by putting on parades, where they dress up in colorful costumes as characters (jonkanoos) from Africa, Great Britain, and the Jamaican political and social scene. On the label is a sketch of a masked jonkanoo. With Jamaican Scotch bonnets, scallions, vinegar, thyme, onions, garlic, sugar, and salt.

West Indian Trinidad Hot Sauce

Trinidad

From Trinidad, heavy with ground habanero chiles, tempered by a little vinegar and spices.

West Indies Creole Classic Red Pepper Sauce

Dominica

Richard Gardner is an anthropologist who in the late 1960s did field work on the "hand-for-hand" labor exchange system in Dominica. He'd bring back pepper sauce, and got so many requests that he decided to bottle it. Tracking down a fifty-year-old island recipe, he started importing the sauce in 1984. Aged with cayenne peppers, herbs, and spices, the sauce resembles a hot, spicy Louisiana sauce, and reflects the Creole influence on Dominica, which was colonized by the French and English. Gardner is still teaching anthropology at San Diego City College, but only part time, since he makes more money with the sauce than he ever made teaching.

West Indies Creole Hot Pepper Sauce

Dominica

Bottled in Red Stripe beer bottles, this sauce is roundly flavored with Scotch bonnets, papayas, onions, vinegar, salt, and spices.

Windmill Hot Pepper Sauce

🌶🌶🌶

Barbados

A beautiful, red-flecked island mustard sauce with habaneros, vinegar, onions, and wheat flour.

Windmill Red Hot Sauce

🌶🌶🌶🌶

Barbados

A thin, red sauce with habaneros, onions, garlic, vinegar, and salt.

Zack's Virgin Habanero Sauce

🌶🌶🌶🌶🌿

Tennessee

Redolent with fresh, yellow habaneros from Jamaica, this sauce is thickened and enlivened with carrots, onions, garlic, lime juice, and spices. It's made by a southerner who has used it as the winning ingredient at chili cookoffs over the last fifteen years.

Louisiana Sauces

Classic Louisiana sauces are a simple blend of cayenne or tabasco peppers, distilled white vinegar, and salt. The peppers and salt are combined to form a mash, which is aged for one to three years, then blended with vinegar. Tabasco is the granddaddy of them all, but hundreds of Louisiana sauces exist, and new takeoffs are appearing, substituting green jalapeños for cayenne peppers, or tweaking the recipe with new ingredients (onions, garlic, and spices) in a cooked, spicy Cajun blend.

This section includes classic Louisiana and Cajun sauces, as well as those from other parts of the world made in that style.

Andre's Rouge Spiced Pepper Sauce

Louisiana

Cajun-born Stan Gauthier has been making hot sauces since 1991, when he got sick of practicing law in Lafayette and decided he'd rather make Cajun foods. With a distinctively spicy flavor, this cayenne and jalapeño pepper sauce is enlivened with brown sugar, garlic, onions, Worcestershire sauce, lemon, butter, and spices.

Another Bloody Day in Paradise Three Pepper Lemon Hot Sauce

Delaware

With 2,600 bottles adorning the walls of his restaurant in Dewey Beach, Chip Hearn may have the world's largest hot sauce collection. He may also have the most popular Bloody Sunday, where up to 1,000 people line up along the boardwalk in the summertime to make Bloody Marys with one of 300 hot sauces. Many choose this house blend, however, which is a bracing combination of chiles (tabasco and green chiles), vinegar, lemon juice, black pepper, and salt. (By the way, if you bring in a sauce Chip hasn't seen, he'll give you a meal on the house.)

Cafe Louisiane Hotter'n Hell Sauce

Louisiana

An aromatic blend of clove, cinnamon, and allspice is added to the traditional Louisiana pepper mash in this spicy sauce. It was created in 1893 by Arthur "Popie" deVillier, a bayou native who cooked in the logging camps of south Louisiana. The Cajun cook became the most important worker at these camps because good food drew the best workers, and camps started competing with each other to have the tastiest food. Popie deVillier's sauce has changed labels in the last few years (it was formerly known as Popie's) and is now called Cafe Louisiane Hotter'n Hell Sauce. Good on gumbos, broiled seafood, and as a marinade for chicken, it has a subtle but lingering warmth.

Cajun Rush XXX Hot Pepper Sauce

🌶️🌶️🌶️🌶️ 🌿 *Louisiana*

With no salt or sugar, this tart, aromatic blend of peppers (cayenne, Asian, and habanero), vinegar, onions, garlic, and a dozen spices is created by Rush Biossat, who—like many sauce makers—began sauce making for friends, who urged him to turn it into a business. In 1992 Rush gave up a career with Ford Motor Company, moved back to his native Louisiana, and got serious about his sauce in Maurepas. He also makes **Cajun Rush Hot Pepper Sauce** (🌶️🌶️🌶️), which is similar but not as hot.

Casa Fiesta Habanero Pepper Sauce

🌶️🌶️🌶️ *Louisiana*

A salty Louisiana-style sauce with habaneros, from Bruce Foods (see page 40).

Chef Hans' Louisiana Hot Sauce

🌶️ *Louisiana*

With a restaurant in Monroe, Chef Hans has been making Creole and Cajun seasonings since 1986. This sauce is driven by cayenne peppers, with a hint of vinegar, salt, and spices. He also makes **Chef Hans' Jalapeno Hot Sauce** (🌶️🌶️), a flavorful sauce that emphasizes the jalapeños over the vinegar and salt.

Chef Paul Prudhomme's Magic Pepper Sauce

Louisiana

From the well-known chef in the French Quarter, this wonderfully balanced Cajun sauce has no aftertaste, with habanero and cayenne peppers, plus vinegar, salt, and spices.

Crystal Hot Sauce

Louisiana

Like many great southern sauce companies, Baumer Foods is proud of its military appeal, and reports that during Desert Storm it was overwhelmed with requests by soldiers to send bottles of Crystal to salvage the mess-hall experience. The Baumer family (which also owns the famed Commander's Palace Restaurant) has been making this simple blend of cayenne peppers, distilled vinegar, and salt since 1923. Crystal's the #3-selling hot sauce in the world (check out the Arabic label) behind Tabasco and Durkee RedHot, commanding 9 percent of market share in supermarkets in 1994.

Crystal Extra Hot Hot Sauce

Louisiana

Similar to Crystal Hot Sauce (with cayenne peppers, distilled vinegar, and salt), but with juiced-up heat.

Dewey Beach Fire Hot Pepper Sauce

 Delaware

From Chip Hearn's Starboard Restaurant in Dewey Beach comes this classic Louisiana hot sauce of cayenne peppers, vinegar, and salt, dressed up with a little garlic and natural flavoring.

Gator Hammock Gator Sauce

Florida

Buddy Taylor lives in a "cough-and-miss-it" hamlet in Florida called Felda (named by Buddy's great grand-father, who in 1923 combined his name of Felix with his wife's name of Ida and came up with Felda). Taylor, who runs the grocery store, had the first satel-lite dish in the area, and on Miami Dolphin weekends invited friends to sports retreats at his 80-foot trailer, perched on a 200-acre homestead. The air was thick with ribs and wings being smoked, then grilled, and always marinated in his sauce, which is named after an alligator in a swamp nearby. With garlic and herbs, this four-year-old sauce is spicier than traditional Louisiana sauces, enlivened with cayenne and crushed red peppers.

Gibbons Louisiana Salsa Picante

Louisiana

A classic Louisiana sauce, with cayenne peppers, vinegar, and a lot of salt.

Goya Hot Sauce

New Jersey

From Goya comes this basic sauce of tabasco peppers, vinegar, and salt, found in ethnic markets from Buffalo to San Juan.

Hot Lava

Florida

Tampa Bay has a number of young hot sauce makers, including Fred Lewis, a Clearwater native who started making salsa in 1990 and peddling it to restaurants from the trunk of his car. When a restaurant ordered 40 gallons, he quit his waiter job, borrowed $3000 from his mother, and went into business. He now produces ten times that amount of salsa daily, as well as this Hot Lava sauce, which has the basic constitution of a Louisiana sauce, although it's thicker and spicier, blended with aged cayenne and Thai peppers, red wine vinegar, salt, and spices.

Louisiana Gold Pepper Sauce

Louisiana

Like Crystal and McIlhenny, Bruce Foods is a family-owned Louisiana hot sauce company. The Brown family established the company in 1928, sending products upriver by paddlewheel boats and horsedrawn wagons. Now, with 1,200 employees, Bruce Foods processes 18 million pounds of peppers annually and sells more than 180 food products (many of them Cajun) in 100 countries worldwide. Their Louisiana Gold has tabasco as well as cayenne peppers.

Original Louisiana Hot Sauce

 Louisiana

Family-owned Bruce Foods is perhaps best known for its Original Louisiana Hot Sauce (cayenne peppers, vinegar, and salt), which was the first pepper sauce marketed under the state's name. I love the straightforward label. They bottle sauce in containers ranging from a two-ounce bottle to a 6,000-gallon tanker truck.

Panola Gourmet Pepper Sauce

Louisiana

Growing up on Panola (his family's plantation in Lake Providence) Grady Brown loved his mother's pepper sauce, a cooked blend of fresh jalapeño and cayenne peppers, vinegar, onions, sugar, salt, and spices. A cotton and rice farmer, Grady decided to bottle the sauce a dozen years ago in an effort to keep his farmhands occupied throughout the winter. This silky sauce took off, and he's now making several sauces, selling upwards of 3 million bottles a year. He even beat out other sauce makers for the military contract for Desert Storm, as well as the 1994 contract for the military. This sauce digresses from the classic Louisiana sauce in that it is cooked, with a blend of spices. Grady also makes **Panola Jalapeno Pepper Sauce** ( ), which is similar to his Gourmet Pepper Sauce, but with fresh, cooked jalapeños.

Panola Cajun Hot Sauce

Louisiana

A sharp sauce of aged pepper mash, vinegar, spices, and salt. Not shown is **Panola Cajun Jalapeno Sauce** ( ), a whistling sauce of aged jalapeño mash, vinegar, and salt.

Panola Extra Hot Sauce

 Louisiana

You can imagine this beautiful Louisiana label on restaurant tables throughout the South. A thin, sharp sauce, with aged pepper mash, vinegar, and salt. A collector's item since the label's been discontinued.

Panola Extra Hot Hot Sauce

Louisiana

With a patriotic red, white, and blue label, this bracing sauce is Panola's third hottest (behind Bat's Brew and Vampfire), made with an aged red pepper mash of tabasco and habanero peppers. (This is the sauce that beat out Tabasco for the 1994 military contract.)

Panola Green
Tabasco Peppers

Louisiana

Bottles of whole peppers steeping in vinegar are popular throughout the South, Central America, and the Caribbean (where they are called piques). This one is made with whole green tabasco peppers, distilled vinegar, and salt.

Pee Wee's Cajun Cayenne Juice

Louisiana

Made by Louisiana-native Stan Gauthier in Breaux Bridge, this sauce is green and medium thick, with a taste that's spicier than hot, but the cayenne and jalapeño peppers come through. Other ingredients include onions, lemon juice, Worcestershire sauce, butter, honey, brown sugar, and spices.

Pee Wee's Green Spiced Pepper Sauce

Louisiana

Identical to Andre's Rouge (see page 36), although immature green cayenne peppers are used instead of mature red ones, giving the sauce a crisp flavor.

Petit Tabasco

El Salvador

This Tabasco imitator from El Salvador adds garlic to the Louisiana blend of chiles, salt, and vinegar.

Red Rooster Louisiana Hot Sauce

Louisiana

A classic Louisiana sauce of cayenne peppers, vinegar, and salt made by family-owned Bruce Foods of New Iberia (see page 40).

San Jorge Pique Tasco

🌶️🌶️🌶️   *Colombia*

Made with tabasco peppers, vinegar, salt, and sugar.

Sho Nuff New Orleans Hot Stuff

🌶️🌶️   *Louisiana*

Russ Cunningham started bottling New Orleans food products back in 1976, and makes this sauce with Louisiana-grown cayenne peppers (many are now grown in South America due to high demand), vinegar, and salt. With the addition of vegetable gum, the sauce is not as runny as some Louisiana sauces, nor is it as salty. Customer loyalty prompted one Canadian stationed in a northern outpost to order a case, and have it sent by UPS to the nearest drop-off point—120 miles away—to which he promptly drove to retrieve the cache.

Southern Spice Jalapeno Hot Sauce

🌶️🌶️🌶️   *Louisiana*

Made by Panola, this sauce of aged jalapeño pepper mash, vinegar, and salt is similar to its Cajun Jalapeno Sauce. Not shown is *Southern Spice Hot Sauce*, (🌶️🌶️🌶️), a classic mash of cayenne peppers, vinegar, and salt, similar to Panola Cajun Hot Sauce (see page 41).

Tabasco Pepper Sauce

Louisiana

Found in more than half of all American households, the family-owned McIlhenny company sells approximately 2 million gallons of Tabasco sauce yearly to over 100 countries. It began when Edmund McIlhenny returned to Avery Island after the Civil War and found that a few of his tabasco pepper plants had survived. He mashed the peppers with salt and let the mixture age for thirty days, then added French wine vinegar and let the flavors blend for a month, at which point he poured the sauce into cologne bottles, corked them, and dipped them with green sealing wax . The year was 1868, and he sold them wholesale for $1 each. The company is rich in history and lore—it was sent to the troops in Europe during World War II, and up into space aboard Skylab. The McIlhenny family was able to secure a trademark on the name, thus eliminating any other "Tabasco" sauces from most of the world market. The peppers are still mashed on Avery Island, although mostly grown elsewhere, and the mash is combined with Avery Island salt and aged in white oak barrels for three years, then blended with vinegar. The sauce is well blended, with the predominant taste that of pepper, not salt. With tabasco peppers hotter than cayenne peppers, Tabasco remains the hottest of the classic Louisiana hot sauces.

Tabasco Jalapeño Sauce

Louisiana

After 125 years, the McIlhenny Company let its hair down a bit and introduced a second sauce, made with ripe jalapeños mixed with vinegar and salt. Milder than the original Tabasco, it's a versatile sauce with a pleasant jalapeño flavor. (McIlhenny also introduced a habanero sauce in the summer of 1995.)

Tasco Chili Pepper Sauce

Guatemala

Imitation is the best form of flattery, as can be seen in this bottle from Guatemala. Over the years, the McIlhenny family has identified a number of hot sauce labels, produced in India, Zaire, Japan, Colombia, Turkey, and Mexico, that have infringed on the diamond-shaped Tabasco trademark. With tabasco peppers, vinegar, and salt.

Trappey's Red Devil Cayenne Pepper Sauce

Louisiana

In the late 1800s, the McIlhenny Company met with substantial competition from other hot sauce makers, including Bernard Trappey (a former blacksmith of Edmund McIlhenny's), who began bottling hot sauce as early as 1896. Trappey's has since been bought by the McIlhenny Company, who continues to produce this salty sauce of cayenne peppers, vinegar, and salt.

Try Me Cajun Sunshine Hot Pepper Sauce

Louisiana

With crushed cayenne peppers, pepper seeds, vinegar, and salt, this popular supermarket sauce is from the Reily Food Company, a Louisiana institution since 1903. It tastes like a thick-bodied Louisiana-style sauce, with plenty of vinegar and salt.

Try Me Tennessee Sunshine Hot Pepper Sauce

Louisiana

In 1989, Reily Food Company purchased the Try Me sauce line from Gourmet Foods in Knoxville. Tennessee Sunshine, which is its #2-seller (next to Tiger Sauce, see page 93), is a Louisiana-style sauce with cayenne and other peppers from California (seeds and all), vinegar, and salt. (The taste is similar to Cajun Sunshine, above). Reily Food employs a homogenizing process to eliminate the problem of vinegar separating and rising to the top of the bottle.

Mexican and Southwestern Sauces

Hot sauces made in Central America and the U.S.

Southwest are often distinguished by the use of a

single pepper—such as the chipotle or pequin—and

often have beautiful brick red colors. Some use

tomatoes, others desert herbs and spices, with the

earthy, sometimes bitter taste of fresh chiles

allowed to emerge. This section includes sauces

made in this style, wherever they are produced.

Achiote Indian Sauce

Pennsylvania

From Hot Heads (page 97) comes this liquid achiote (achiote is a hard, red bean derived from the annato seed, used widely throughout Central and South America as a natural dye and food coloring), which is blended with tepin chiles, vinegar, natural herbs, and spices.

ACME Almost Flammable Hot Sauce

New York

Many people are private-labeling existing sauces, such as the Acme Bar & Grill in New York (a roadhouse with a great hot sauce collection), whose house brand bears a strong resemblance to the fiery Mexican El Yucateco sauce (page 55), and comes in bright red (not shown) or shocking green. This bar is so dedicated to hot sauces that the tables are painted to look like giant hot sauce labels. With habaneros, vinegar, tomatoes, salt, and spices.

Adobe Milling Jalapeño Hot Sauce

Colorado

Made with vine-ripened jalapeños, vinegar, and salt, this beautiful reddish brown sauce is from a bean company in Dove Creek best known for reintroducing an heirloom bean called the anasazi to the market. Nothing beats hot sauce on rice and beans, and so their segue from beans to sauce seemed natural.

Aji Amazona Aji Verde en Vinagre

Colombia

This sauce bottles whole green Amazon peppers in salt. Grown in Colombia, Amazon peppers rate about 55–80,000 scoville units, slightly hotter than tabasco chiles.

Aji Amazona Salsa Roja Picante

Colombia

Made with red Amazon peppers, salt, and vinegar, this sauce is imported by a produce man from Virginia who's involved in shipping bananas and vegetables from Colombia, and discovered this sauce on a business trip. Not shown is *Aji Amazona Salsa Verde Picante* (), which is similar, but with green Amazon peppers.

America's Cup '95 Hot Sauce

California

Andrew Keeler is a hot sauce collector who has been known to mail hot sauces with holiday labels instead of Christmas cards to friends. Living in San Diego, he thought that hot sauce could commemorate the city's biggest sports event: the America's Cup Race. Making an arrangement with the makers of Juanita's sauce (page 57), he designed the label and sold the sauce around town. Given their increasing popularity (not to mention the fact that they are inexpensive and pocket-sized), custom-labeled sauces make an ideal souvenir or party giveaway.

Ana Belly Extra Salsa Picante Hot Sauce

Guatemala

A thin-flavored sauce of dried chiles, vinegar, and salt that doesn't benefit from its plastic bottle.

Arizona Gunslinger Smokin' Hot Jalapeño Pepper Sauce

Arizona

This earthy red sauce made with red, ripe jalapeños, vinegar, and salt was created in 1987, when two golfing buddies grew too many jalapeños. Like many sauce stories, Arizona Gunslinger was bottled at home in the kitchen until 1990, when sales started soaring. Arizona Gunslinger now casts its net as far as Japan.

Ass Kickin' Hot Sauce

Arizona

Also from Arizona, this tangy sauce provides a billowing, middle-of-the-mouth heat from the red serranos and habaneros, which are blended with fresh onions, fresh garlic, and spices in a tomato base.

Aztexan Pepper Co. Habanero Supreme Hot Sauce

🌶️🌶️🌶️🌶️ 🌿   *Texas*

Thin as a Louisiana sauce but flavored with habaneros, onions, carrots, garlic, vinegar, lime juice, and salt, this pretty, ocher-colored sauce with burning back-of-the-mouth heat comes from Mark Witt, an Austin caterer who serves musicians along 6th Street in the wee hours from his catering van. He always sets out hot sauces, plus his homemade sauce, which keeps getting stolen. "We even tried chaining the bottle to the van, but with no success." He entered the Austin Hot Sauce contest in 1993—a huge affair that draws thousands of people—and took first place in the specialty division. He grows his own habaneros for the sauce.

Brazos Beef Emporium Cowboy Cayenne Pepper Sauce

🌶️🌶️   *Texas*

Craig Conlee is from an old Texas family—his father was sheriff of Brazos County and his grandmother cooked for the guys in jail. This family recipe, which they started bottling in 1985, has cayenne peppers, vinegar, and salt.

Brown Adobe Oso Hot!

🌶️🌶️🌶️🌶️ 🌿   *Pennsylvania*

Scorching from habaneros, earthy from New Mexico red chiles, and faintly sweet with red wine vinegar and garlic, this smooth sauce conjures up the flavors of the Southwest. While they were courting, Julienne Brown's New Mexican husband won her heart by sending her New Mexico green and red chiles. (Is this a trend among hot sauce makers? Isla Vieques maker Jim Starke won his Rhode Island wife's heart by mailing her papayas from the Caribbean.) By the time the Browns moved East, Julienne was addicted to chiles, and had her in-laws send shipments to her. Oso means bear in Spanish, and is also a symbol of good health.

Bustelo's Chipotle Pepper Sauce

🌶️🌶️🌶️🌿   *California*

Manufacturers often make sample batches of sauces they plan to introduce to the market, testing them on friends and in labs to determine their shelf life (to make sure they don't explode, among other things). The lead time for Larry Watson's products is a year (see page 80), which is the amount of time he ages his sauces in white oak casks. A thick, full-flavored, velvety, smoky sauce.

Castillo Salsa Habanera

🌶️🌶️🌶️🌶️   *Mexico*

Family made in Mexico since the early 1940s, this fiery sauce is flavored with habaneros from the Yucatan penin-sula, in a base of red tomatoes, vinegar, and spices. Castillo contains no flour or starch as thickeners. They also make a similar sauce (also called **Castillo Salsa Habanera** 🌶️🌶️🌶️🌶️), that uses green, unripe haban-eros for a slightly tangier taste.

Cholula Hot Sauce

🌶️🌶️🌶️   *Mexico*

From Jalisco, this smooth sauce has been made for three generations by the same family in Cholula, a town not too far from Puebla. From the rare pequín pepper, plus vinegar, salt, and spices, Cholula makes a fine marinade for meats and grilled vegetables, and it sports the best cap on the market. Imported by Jalisco Food Company of San Antonio.

Coyote Cocina Smoky Chipotle Sauce

New Mexico

From chef Mark Miller and the Coyote Cafe of Santa Fe comes this rich, earthy, smoky sauce with a light vinegar finish. A consummate blend of chipotle chiles, pasilla negro chiles, fresh garlic, and spices. He also makes **Coyote Cocina Tangy Taco Sauce** ( ), which blends New Mexico red chiles with red wine vinegar, salt, and spices in a tangy beautifully colored sauce.

Daytona Bike Week Hot Sauce

Florida

Douglas Feindt developed hot sauces while captaining oil rig supply boats, and U.S. Navy research vessels. "I was the Captain, but couldn't stay out of the galley. I was always a chef at heart." This crisp sauce of habaneros, carrots, onions, vinegar, garlic, lime juice, and salt was made for Daytona Bike Week, the world's largest motorcycle event.

Desert Fire Hot Sauce

Arizona

Fragrant with thyme and other dried herbs of the Southwest, this thick, deep-hued sauce blends crushed serranos (seeds and all) in a hearty, spicy tomato base. From Southwest Specialty Food Company.

Diaguitas Ají

Chile

An organic blend of ají chiles and salt from the Elqui Valley of Chile. While *ají* is Spanish for chile peppers, it also refers to a South American pepper, *capsicum baccatum*. The natural soil conditions in the high desert of the Andes, with no rainfall in this valley, are perfect for the ají, allowing farmers to preserve the peppers without chemicals. An ancient pepper, it has long been used medicinally by Indians and is slightly hotter than the tabasco pepper. Essentially a chile extract, this sauce is hot, salty, and slightly bitter, and is delicious in Bloody Marys.

Dr. J's Habanero Chile Elixir

New Mexico

Dr. J is a microbiologist who works with natural products that enhance plant growth. He's also a Cajun and a gardener who was introduced to habaneros by Dr. Ben Villalon, a breeder of chile varieties, after boasting that no chile was too hot. Obtaining seeds from Villalon, Dr. J started growing habaneros and making sauce. In the early 1980s he was teaching a course in fermentation, and found a fermenting process other than that used in Louisiana sauces; his sauce is fermented with a special yeast he's isolated and developed, giving his sauce a unique flavor. It's a tasty blend of habanero and red chiles, vinegar, and salt. Every bottle is dated.

Ducal Hot Sauce

Guatemala

Simply hot peppers, water, salt, and starch.

El Gallero Salsa Picante

🌶️🌶️🌶️   *Mexico*

Made with de arbol chiles (similar to cayenne peppers), vinegar, and salt.

El Yucateco

🌶️🌶️🌶️🌶️   *Yucatan*

A delicious, slightly thick, grainy sauce with a quick heat and mild vinegar finish, made with immature green habaneros. "This hot sauce was born with the wish of one very nice hot sauce for everybody," said company president Jose Gamboa, who has been making it for twenty years and is very interested in Mayan culture. From the Yucatan, the habaneros are milled with spices, then cooked and bottled. You can often find El Yucateco sauces on tables in Mexican restaurants—it's the one with an other-worldly green color reminiscent of engine coolant. They also make a red *El Yucateco* (🌶️🌶️🌶️🌶️), which is similar to the green El Yucateco, but with red habaneros from the Yucatan.

Endorphinator Mango BBQ Sauce

🌶️🌶️🌶️🌿   *Texas*

Wow! From David Garrido at Jeffrey's Restaurant in Austin comes this smoky, irresistible sauce that skilfully combines chipotles with mangos, mustard, celery, brown sugar, and horseradish.

Fire in the Hole Habanera Hot Sauce

🌶🌶🌶   *Texas*

A quick-fire blend of habaneros, vinegar, salt, and onions.

Fish Camp Habanero Sauce

🌶🌶🌶🌿   *Austin*

This collector's item was chef David Garrido's house sauce at Fish Camp, a lakeside restaurant in Austin now called the Marina Cafe. It's a sweet-spicy blend of apple cider vinegar, tomatoes, carrots, onions, celery, honey, habaneros, garlic, lemon, and spices.

Hot Sauce Harry's Dynamite Hot Sauce

🌶🌶🌶   *Texas*

Advertising executive Bob Harris took a flavorful Caribbean-style sauce of habaneros, carrots, onions, vinegar, garlic, lime juice, and salt, and gave it a Texas identity with various labels, including Hot Sauce Harry's Dynamite (which comes in a "firecracker" case), **Fort Worth Flame**, **Hot Sauce Harry's Habanero Hot Sauce**, **Texas Firecracker**, and **Bob Harris Hot Ideas Hot Sauce**. It's a good example of how regional distinctions break down as sauces are transported and changed over time. Hot sauce lovers, Bob and his wife Dianne in 1994 opened Hot Sauce Harry's, a hot sauce booth at the Dallas Farmer's Market.

Juanita's Picante Hot Sauce

 California

Juanita's Foods is a family-run company (and the world's largest maker of menudo), founded in California in 1946 (originally called Harbor Canning Company), that makes authentic Mexican food. A mellow sauce with a nice, dried red chile finish and a lovely lady on the label.

La Botanera

Mexico

Thick as relish, this salty sauce has red peppers, safflower oil, citric acid, herbs, and spices.

La Guaca—Maya Botanera

Mexico

The cora pepper is featured in this smooth blend of water, lemon, salt, and spices. The bottle features the company's trademark parrot.

La Sabroza Chile de Arbol

Mexico

Long, thin, and slightly tannic, the de arbol chile is referred to as *pico de pajaro* because it resembles a bird's beak. Made in Monterrey, Mexico, since 1991, this mild, tangy sauce is good as a condiment for tacos, sautéed meats, and enchiladas. Not shown is **La Sabroza Chipotle** (   ), where the flavor of the chipotles (jalapeños that have been smoked) shines through. Blended with tomatoes, onions, salt, and spices, the sauce has no vinegar, which can sometimes make chipotle sauces too tart.

Lizano Chile

Costa Rica

Found on most restaurant tables in Costa Rica, a simple sauce of chiles, water, and salt. Lizano also makes a **Chilero** hot sauce with cayenne peppers and tomato paste, and a **Tabasco** sauce with tabasco chiles, water, and salt. (Interestingly, as long as Lizano doesn't sell its Tabasco sauce outside Costa Rica, the sauce is not an infringement on McIlhenny's Tabasco trademark.)

Lol-Tun Habanero Peppers Hot Sauce

Mexico

Bright flecks of spices float in this deliciously tangy sauce of habaneros, vinegar, carrots, onions, and spices.

Mar Isquera

                     Mexico

Made with the guajillo chile, a mild Mexican chile with
berry accents. Other ingredients include water, salt,
and vinegar.

Mayan Kut

Pennsylvania

From the Hot Heads folks who offer you Last Rites (see
page 97) comes an interesting Mexican sauce spiked with
jalapeños and habaneros, sweetened with brown sugar
and raisins, and enlivened with lime juice. Makers
Wendy and Kenny Roda spend part of each year in the
Yucatan, and learned to make this generations-old sauce
from Mayan Indians.

The Mean Green

Mexico

An unadulterated blend of green habaneros, salt,
and vinegar, made for Hot Heads (see above) in the
Yucatan.

The Mex Hot Sauce

🌶🌶🌶 🌿
Maine

From a restaurant in northern Maine that features regional Mexican cooking comes this purée of jalapeño, serrano, pasilla, and cayenne peppers, plus dried Mexican chiles.

Mezzetta California Twist & Shout Habanero Hot Sauce

🌶🌶🌶
California

Sonoma, California, is not exactly the Southwest, but this sauce—a blend of habaneros and other peppers, tomato paste, vinegar, salt, spices, and herbs—is similar to many found along the border. Mezzetta also makes **Mezzetta California Hot Sauce** (🌶🌶), which is similar but not as hot (with California hot peppers instead of habaneros), and with tomato purée instead of tomato paste. Both have a strong tomato flavor.

Montezuma Aztec Hot Sauce

🌶🌶 🌿
Ohio

Montezuma sauces hail from Ohio, where sauce maker/collector Chuck Evans is committed to making authentic Mexican-style sauces. He became interested in southwestern culture while traveling with his church youth group, then spent a summer running a Bible school on a Navajo reservation in Arizona. Pre-Colombian in origin, this Aztec style hot sauce is found in corked liquor bottles in marketplaces of northern and west central Mexico. It's made with the de arbol chile, along with native spices, garlic, cider vinegar, sesame seeds, pumpkin seeds (for flavoring and thickening), and salt.

Montezuma Habañero Hot Hot Hot Sauce

🌶️🌶️🌶️🌶️ 🌿

Ohio

Available in green or red, this spicy sauce blends habaneros, garlic, and spices.

Montezuma Wild Pequín Hot Sauce

🌶️🌶️🌶️ 🌿

Ohio

Grown in the wild and hand cultivated, pequín chiles have a fierce bite. This sauce of distilled and cider vinegar, salt, spices, and pequíns, is typical of northern Mexican sauces from Sonora to Nuevo Leon. Montezuma sauces not shown include **Montezuma Chile Cascabel Hot Sauce** (🌶️), a simple sauce made with the nutty cascabel ("little bell" in Spanish) chile from north-central Mexico, garlic, vinegar, water, and salt; **Montezuma Smokey Chipotle Hot Sauce** (🌶️🌶️) which has an assertive chipotle flavor (and a touch of pasilla negro chiles), with a strong vinegar finish; and **Montezuma Smokey Chipotle Habanero Hot Sauce** (🌶️🌶️🌶️), which combines Montezuma chipotle and habanero sauces, creating a sauce that is smoky-sweet and rather herbal.

Ozone Shooter Tomatillo Serrano Sauce

🌶️🌶️ 🌿

Texas

Fresh tomatillos are evident in this seductive sauce of poblanos, serranos, habaneros, onions, and garlic, complemented by cilantro. From Jeffrey's Restaurant in Austin, a portion of the sauce proceeds are donated to Share Our Strength.

Pasa Salsa Picante

🌶️🌶️🌶️🌶️   *San Salvador*

A startlingly hot and lingering sauce of habaneros, dried
red peppers, vinegar, and salt.

Pico Pica Hot Sauce

🌶️🌶️   *California*

Established in 1937, Pico Pica was the first Mexican-
style hot sauce made in Los Angeles. An aromatic
tomato-based blend of chiles, salt, spices, vegetable oil,
and garlic powder, this smooth red sauce is one of
David Letterman's favorites.

Ring of Fire
Habeñero Hot Sauce

🌶️🌶️🌶️🌿   *California*

A fresh-tasting sauce from San Diego, filled with the flavor of tomatoes, onions, and roasted garlic, plus
habanero and roasted serrano chiles. Not ones to skimp
on quality, Michael Greening and Diane Matsunage
blend it with Four Monks White Wine Vinegar. They also
make **Ring of Fire X-tra Hot Reserve Habeñero Hot
Sauce** (🌶️🌶️🌶️🌶️), which has similar ingredients,
but is hotter. The sauce comes with a "crying towel" (the
cloth covering the neck). One fan wrote that to taste
their sauce and then continue to use a cheap supermarket brand "would be like drinking a Sanka expres-
so." No, sanka.

Rio Diablo Hot Sauce

🌶️🌶️ 🌿   *Texas*

Smoky from the start, this salsa-like sauce is rich with tomatoes, garlic, lime juice, spices, and jalapeños that have been smoked over a mesquite fire for up to 12 hours (leaving them plump and juicy, but with a resolute smokiness). After Joe Dulle won the 1993 Austin Hot Sauce Contest, he decided to bottle the sauce, which was born out of necessity while trying to complement the venison that's found in the Hill Country outside Austin. He also makes a Rio Diablo Mesquite-Smoked Hot Sauce with chipotles.

Salsa Huichol Hot Sauce

🌶️🌶️🌶️ 🌿   *Mexico*

This particularly rich-tasting Mexican sauce is made with cascabel peppers from the Nayar Mountains, combined with vinegar, salt, and spices. The dried chiles give the sauce a smooth, red finish, which makes the slow buildup of heat even more startling.

Santa Cruz Green Salsa

🌶️🌶️🌶️ 🌿   *Arizona*

This savory sauce of jalapeños, green chiles (seeds included), onions, carrots, garlic, vinegar, and spices is made by a family-owned company a few miles north of the Mexican border in Tumacacori. Juliet Kibbey England was born on a cattle ranch in Sonora, Mexico, and was married for years to an Arizona cattle rancher. She started a ranch museum at the Santa Cruz Chili & Spice Company with related memorabilia (her husband was involved in early aviation, which is also on display), and her food products highlight the authentic flavors of the Santa Cruz valley.

Santa Fe Olé 3 Pepper Hot Sauce

New Mexico

This tasty sauce blends three peppers (chipotles, New Mexico reds, and red jalapeños) in a rich, smoky, spicy sauce with cider vinegar, garlic, cumin, and salt. Maker Martin Dobyns started with two pots in his kitchen in 1985, and now makes twenty items that utilize New Mexico chiles and capture the region's culinary diversity.

Shotgun Willie's 2-Barrel Habanero Pepper Sauce

Texas

Dan and Lisa Jardine started in their Austin kitchen in 1979 with $5000, and now head D.L. Jardine's, a company with over 100 food products and sales topping $5 million in 1992. The company is nestled in a 30-acre ranch in Texas with oak rocking chairs on the porch and mesquite trees along the driveway. Slightly more complex than a Louisiana sauce, this vinegar-based blend includes cayenne, jalapeno, and tabasco peppers, plus salt.

S.O.B.

Pennsylvania

Warning: S.O.B. can alter facial expressions and cause strong vocabulary, but don't let it scare you. Made with crushed habanero peppers, vinegar, tomatoes, and spices by Hot Heads (see page 97).

Tamazula Salsa Picante

Mexico

A smooth, rich, red chile sauce from Guadalajara, made simply with peppers, vinegar, salt, and spices.

"Tapatío"

California

The dried red chiles send heat immediately to the roof of your mouth in this smooth, orange sauce with spices and a bit of sugar.

Texapeppa Jalapeno Sauce

Texas

Bright green, this jalapeño purée made with spices by D.L. Jardine's (see page 64) is good on eggs, home fries, or pizza.

Texas Champagne Pepper Sauce

Texas

With aged red peppers, vinegar, and salt, from D.L. Jardine's, proudly Texan.

"Texas Sweat" Jalapeño Juice

Texas

A versatile jalapeño sauce, with vinegar and salt.

Texas Terminator Habanero Sauce

Texas

From David Garrido at Jeffrey's Restaurant in Austin, a thick habanero sauce that starts out sweet then sneaks up to a midlevel heat and loads of flavor. With tomatoes, carrots, onions, celery, habaneros, vinegar, cilantro, honey, lemon, garlic, and spices.

Tia Juana

Mexico

Shaped like bullets, serrano chiles have a lasting heat and a sharp, vegetable-like flavor. Here they are cooked with salt, vinegar, and spices.

Trappey's Mexi-Pep Hot Sauce

Louisiana

Trappey's (now owned by McIlhenny, page 45) has been a Louisiana institution since 1896. A simple border sauce, made with three kinds of peppers (cayenne, jalapeño and tabasco) plus vinegar and salt.

Try Me Yucatan Sunshine Habanero Pepper Sauce

Louisiana

Found in grocery stores nationwide, the habanero heat of this sauce made by the Reily Food Company (see page 46) is controlled by the addition of carrots, onions, vinegar, garlic, lime juice, and salt.

Other Continents

While chile peppers originated in the Americas—as did pepper sauces (which the Spanish found Indians cooking with when they landed in the Caribbean)—other continents have developed their own styles of hot sauce as chiles made their way around the world. Throughout Asia and Africa, in particular, fiery sauces are an integral component of the culinary architecture, and the brands and varieties probably outnumber occidental sauces. This section includes sauces from Asia, Africa, and Europe, as well as sauces made in the traditions of these continents.

Adriatic Hot Ajvar

🌶️🌶️🌶️🌶️ 🌿   *Slovenia*

From Slovenia comes this neon orange ajvar (sauce) in an industrial sized bottle with peppers, eggplant, garlic, spices, and salt. It is mildly spicy, with the eggplant and roasted red peppers predominating.

Berrak Aci Biber Sosu

🌶️🌶️🌶️   *Turkey*

This salty relish of a sauce (sosu), with peppers, olive oil, vinegar, and salt, is good spread on meats or hamburgers.

Brother Bru-Bru's African Hot Sauce

🌶️🌶️🌶️🌶️ 🌿   *California*

Would you believe that this sauce is made by Mr. Tamborine Man? Bruce Langhorne (aka Brother Bru Bru) is a musician who worked with Bob Dylan, and is indeed Mr. Tamborine Man. A few years ago, Bruce was told by his doctor to eliminate salt, and so—already addicted to hot sauces—he started blending peppers. As a player of African music (with Hugh Masekela and others), and a lover of African cultures, he started using African spices. Salt free, this stinging sauce has habanero, Asian japone, and African bird peppers blended with garlic, West African spices, and lots of apple cider vinegar. "These spices don't have English names," he explained, having taken samples of the spices to friends at the USDA, who were able to identify them in old scholarly texts, so now he knows the Latin names in addition to the Ibo and Yoruba names. He also makes a mild salt-free version with tomatoes called ***Brother Bru-Bru's Mild African Hot Sauce*** (🌶️).

Candido Piri Piri

 France

From France, a blend of pepper pulp with vinegar. This sauce is often called piri piri in Europe and pili pili in Africa.

Cosmopolitan Sambal Wayang Bawang Putih

 New Jersey

With chunks of garlic, this Indonesian sambal is slightly sweet and spicy, with sweet soy sauce, onions, spices, and lemon. With no salt, it's made by Cosmopolitan Food's Nick ten Velde, an Indonesian who moved to the United States via the Netherlands, and started making authentic sambals in 1983 (see page 104), with Chinese, Indian, and Indonesian chiles, all imported from the Far East. He also makes *Cosmopolitan Sambal Wayang Kerrie* ( ), a salt-free curried (kerrie) sambal with Far Eastern chiles, plus onions, lemon, curry, and spices.

Dilijan Liquid Spice

New Jersey

More a cooking ingredient than a sauce, this ruby-colored liquid spice is made with just soy oil and a natural extract of fresh chile peppers. It makes a good substitute for dried chile powder, with 1/4 teaspoon of sauce equaling 1/4 teaspoon of cayenne powder or 1 teaspoon of fresh chopped jalapeños.

Goldwin Garlic Chilli Sauce

Singapore

A mild garlic sauce with red chiles, distilled vinegar, garlic, and salt.

Harissa Dea

France

Served with couscous, this chile paste made with the cayenne pepper (called the "enraged pepper" in French), is popular in North Africa and France. This heat-driven blend includes vegetables, vegetable oil, salt, coriander, caraway, and garlic.

Harissa Le Flambeau du Cap Bon

Tunisia

With pimientos, garlic, and oriental spices, this hot Tunisian paste is often diluted liberally in the cooking sauce, then served over couscous.

Huy Fong Sambal Oelek

California

A bright red sauce of chiles, vinegar, and salt.

Huy Fong Túóng Ót Sriracha Hot Chili Sauce

California

Huy Fong is a fifteen-year-old Los Angeles company, whose first product was a pepper saté sauce. Its Vietnamese Sriracha Hot Chili sauce—with the cocky emblem and the plastic squeeze bottle—has a cult following and fiercely loyal fans, particularly among inmates, Huy Fong reports. Made with fresh red jalapeño peppers, vinegar, garlic, sugar, and salt, it's a zesty garlic-driven chile sauce. They also make ***Huy Fong Túóng Ót Tói Viet-Nam*** ( ), a thick, garlic sauce with chiles, vinegar, and salt.

Jo B's Chile Granatus Hot Chile Sambal

Vermont

This Indonesian-style relish (sambal) made in Vermont has a fresh green chile flavor, which is tempered (slightly) with fresh lime juice and garlic—nothing else.

Jufran "Pam-Pa-Gana" Banana Sauce

Philippines

A mild sauce from Manila with bananas, vinegar, sugar, salt, spices, and chiles.

Lee Kum Kee Singaporean Chili Sauce

Hong Kong

Lee Kum Kee grew out of a small Chinese oyster sauce business founded in 1888 in China's southern Guangdong Province. Now relocated to Hong Kong, the family business is run by fourth generation sauce makers who produce over sixty hot sauces under the Lee Kum Kee and Panda brand names. This sauce was formulated for Singaporean cuisine, with a vinegary aroma, and ginger flavor. Their **Lee Kum Kee Chili Oil** ( ) is a blend of red chiles and vegetable oil. **Lee Kum Kee Sweet Chili Sauce** ( ) is sweetened with plums.

Macarico Piri-Piri

Portugal

Piri piri is thought to be derived from the African pili pili, which is not only a small hot African pepper (the name is a bastardization of the Arabic felfel, or strong pepper), but also a sauce that is traditionally made by crushing the peppers with a tomato paste. This Portuguese sauce is made by steeping piri piri pulp in brine (salt).

Mida's Chilli Sauce

India

From Calcutta, chiles, vinegar, and spices, in a thick, fragrant sauce.

Mongo Hot Sauce

 *Illinois*

You can see and taste the sesame seeds and soy sauce in this earthy red sauce that's blended with jalapeño and Chinese cayenne peppers, vinegar, onions, sugar, sesame oil, and garlic powder.

Noh Korean Hot Sauce

Hawaii

This Korean sauce includes soy bean paste and soy sauce in a blend of chiles, vinegar, honey, rice sugar, onions, and garlic.

Panda Brand Lee Kum Kee Hot Chili Sauce

Hong Kong

Lots of garlic in this thick sauce of red, ripened jalapeños, sugar, and salt, from a fourth generation of sauce makers in Hong Kong (see page 72).

Panda Brand Lee Kum Kee Sambal Oelek

Hong Kong

A thick, seeded relish with a lingering heat from red jalapeño peppers, sugar, spices, and plenty of salt. Lee Kum Kee also produces **Panda Sriracha Chili Sauce** ( ), with the same ingredients and garlic.

Pantainorasingh Sweet Chilli Sauce

Thailand

Notable ingredients in this mild sauce include fermented garlic and maize flower, which are blended with unfermented garlic, red chiles, salt, sugar, and water. The label says it's good on "shrimp, crab, cuttlefish, and cockleshell."

Pili Hot Pepper Condiment

Washington, D.C.

This sauce was created by a hairstylist and diplomat who missed the fiery flavors of Zaire. Haitian-born Paul Lochard—who has cut Richard Burton's locks—and his diplomat wife Beverly were stationed in Zaire, and fell in love with the spicy African condiment pili. When work brought her to Washington, they decided to create their own. Paul had grown up with *sauce ti malice* ("bad little sauce" in Haiti), and the two perfected a recipe by grinding red habaneros and onions, frying the blend in corn oil, and mixing it with tomato paste, garlic, and lemon juice (no vinegar). They ran a design contest for the label with a university art department, and introduced their sauce to the market in three heat levels.

Pyramid Brand
Red Pepper Sauce

🌶️🌶️   *Turkey*

Just puréed peppers, lots of salt, and
preservatives, from Turkey.

Selin Hot
Pepper Souce

🌶️🌶️   *Turkey*

This Turkish "souce" is thick and dense
with pimientoes and salt. Mild, tran-
sient heat.

Tommy Tang's Seracha
Chili Pepper Sauce

🌶️🌶️🌿   *Thailand*

Restaurateur Tommy Tang bottles this garlicky sauce
with Thai chiles, vinegar, natural sea salt, and sugar.

Wajang Sambal Oelek

🌶 🌶   *Holland*

Given the importance of the Netherlands along the
trade routes in the 1500s, it's not surprising to see an
Indonesian sambal from Holland, with peppers and
vinegar.

Ziyad Hot Red Pepper Sauce

🌶 🌶   *Turkey*

Thick with seeds, this sauce is a blend of
Turkish red peppers, salt, and sunflower oil.

The Melting Pot

In many ways, traditional regional distinctions are being overshadowed by the sheer mobility of people and the availability of ingredients. Borrowing from many traditions, these sauces can't be easily pigeonholed—a spirited blend of worldly ingredients sets apart this eclectic group.

Atlanta Burning Sauce

🌶🌶🌶   *Georgia*

A woody, smoky flavor is evident upon uncapping this sauce, a seamless blend of cayenne peppers, tomatoes, brown sugar, natural smoke flavor, apple cider vinegar, and tamarind. Atlanta Burning has been around for twenty-five years as a rib sauce, and has recently entered the hot sauce arena.

Batten Island Extra Hot Gourmet Sauce

🌶🌶🌶 🌿   *Florida*

A generous, fruity flavor is apparent immediately from the applesauce, dates, prunes, and pears in this dark, intense sauce blended with habaneros, cayenne peppers, tomato paste, brown sugar, and onions. It's made by a Florida ostrich farmer, who even makes an ostrich jerky with the sauce.

Bat's Brew Hot Sauce

🌶🌶🌶🌶   *Louisiana*

A whimsically named sauce from Panola, makers of many Louisiana-style sauces (see page 41). Their hottest, this sauce combines habanero and red jalapeño peppers with onions, sugar, spices, and lemon oil.

Bill Wharton's Liquid Summer

🌶️🌶️🌶️

Florida

Bill Wharton is a hot blues man, whose slide guitar and band—The Ingredients—are well known to Florida blues fans. One of the few music acts in the country where the musicians cook gumbo for the audience, "The Sauce Boss" is a capsicum-lover's snake oil salesman, and his fans love it. Liquid Summer features the datil pepper, which Wharton discovered while playing gigs in St. Augustine. A seamless blend of tomatoes, vinegar, garlic, onions, olive oil, sugar, and spices, with the high notes provided by the datils.

Bone Suckin' Sauce

North Carolina

A sweet, rich barbecue cross-dresser with reticent heat, consummately blending tomato paste, honey, and horseradish with lemon juice, natural hickory smoke flavor, and local peppers. Created in the western North Carolina style, it's good served straight up on ribs, chicken, or game.

Bourbon Street Fire Sauce

🌶️🌶️🌶️

Vermont

Confetti-sized jalapeño chunks are blended harmoniously with vinegar, honey, garlic, herbs, spices, lemon juice, and Worcestershire sauce in this intense sauce with the consistency of relish. From chef Arthur O'Connor at the Bourbon Street Grill, a heat-seeking restaurant in Burlington, Vermont.

Bubba Brand H'eatin Hot Sauce

 .   *South Carolina*

The South meets the Southwest and Caribbean in this delicious sauce of chipotles, habaneros, and sweet potatoes, rounded out with onions, vinegar, and spices. "Bubbas aren't afraid of a little heat," claims its maker. "They spend hours attached to fishing poles out on aluminum boats in the hottest part of the summer." Check out the Acme radiator on the label.

Bustelo's Very Hot Pepper Sauce

          California

Larry Watson is a mechanical design engineer who settled in Sonoma County and on the side started making this fine hot sauce, employing cooking styles that were intended as a tongue-in-cheek send up of the wine folks. He'd carefully blend perfect proportions of red, white, and rice vinegars, then experiment with chiles that would fill the mouth ("from a chipotle bass to a habanero top note"). After making his Bustelo's sauce, he aged it in white oak barrels for a year, and discovered a principle of wine making: He could marry the flavors in oak. "When I bottled my sauce and shared it with my wine friends," recalls Larry, "they were delighted, and proclaimed that 'Bustelo has a big nose, a full mouth, and a long finish.' It took me two years to realize that they were talking about me, not the sauce!" They were also amazed at the complexity of flavors, and shared knowledge and resources with him. This sauce is an earthy, fragrant blend of chiles, vinegar, garlic and salt. Larry also makes **Bustelo's Habanero Pepper Sauce** ( ) which is a youthful blend with a ripe, generous habanero flavor and hot finish.

Calido Chile Traders Besos de Fuego Pepper Sauce

Kansas

With a hint of apples, this smooth "kiss of fire" is made with habaneros, Dijon mustard, apples, prepared mustard, garlic, spices, lemon juice, and sugar. (The sauce was formerly known as Lotta Hotta Besos de Fuego until a lawsuit forced the company to change its name; the original sauce is now strictly a collector's item.) The sauce is made by Calido Chile Traders, a company formed by two Kansas City buddies who opened the first of several Mexican restaurants in 1980 and challenged the regulars to try their hot sauces. Next came a store featuring the sauces—and they've recently franchised the hot shop concept, with stores nationwide.

California Perfect Pepper Sauce

California

Craig Bigelow started bottling salsa in 1987 while owner of The Head of the Wolf Restaurant. In Santa Barbara, he recently branched into this mild, chunky sauce, flavored with jalapeños, garlic, onions, olive oil, vinegar, and spices.

Captain Redbeard's Olde Florida Hot Sauce

Florida

With a hint of cilantro, this sauce from a Florida tugboat captain also has aged red cayenne peppers, vinegar, lime juice, garlic, and spices.

Century Habanero Pepper Sauce

Ohio

From an insurance executive in Ohio who cooks by night, this Caribbean-inspired sauce hints of tomatoes, with red habaneros, onions, garlic, and spices. Sauce maker Kathleen Redle also makes **Century Hot Pepper Sauce** (   ), which hits you first with the flavor of tomatoes and spices, then gives a delayed quick blast from the cayenne and Thai peppers, which are grown organically in Ohio by retired Catholic Dominican nuns. Other ingredients include tomato paste and fresh garlic.

Chesapeake Bay Habanero Hot Sauce

St. Thomas

A tart, vegetable-filled sauce with roots in the Chesapeake, where Matthew Cobb grew up and came to love seafood seasoning blends, but with an island twist (where Cobb now lives) that combines tomatoes, bell peppers, and onions with Jamaican chocolate, habaneros, honey, lemon juice, and Chesapeake seasonings. Cobb created this sauce with seafood in mind, and it's delicious with things that swim as well as crawl.

Chile Today Hot Tamale Original Smoked Habanero Gourmet Hot Sauce

New Jersey

Step-brothers in New Jersey founded Chile Today Hot Tamale, a terrific hot sauce and chile pepper-of-the-month club. They started their business four years ago by ordering two pounds of peppers, which they strung and sold as ristras. They grind most of their chiles into powder on demand, which makes it hotter and fresher than many dried chile powders. They've recently entered the hot sauce market with this clean, intense sauce that features pasilla and smoked habanero chiles, deftly blended with papayas, onions, lemon juice, and garlic.

Clancy's Fancy Hot Sauce

Michigan

Often small, odd-shaped bottles are a good indication that a sauce is made fresh in small batches. Colleen Clancy is an Irishwoman from Knockmaroon Gate who attended convent school, where she met students from Trinidad, the Sudan, and India, who shared condiments to enliven boarding school fare. Fifteen years later in Ann Arbor, she borrowed on various culinary traditions to create this supple blend of first-pressed green olive oil, cayenne and sweet peppers, soya mineral bouillon, raw Michigan honey, fresh organic garlic, ginger root, and apple cider vinegar.

Creative Chef Hot Peppered Orange Sauce

Missouri

Sweet and sour flavors compete in this jammy sauce filled with bits of lemon, garlic, and red habaneros, blended with orange juice. Good with game or smoked meats, this sauce also benefits from the addition of a hefty splash of Jack Daniels to make a bourbon barbecue sauce.

Dave's Insanity Sauce II, The Second Burning

California

An exuberant, bracing blend of horseradish, habanero and de arbol chiles, ketchup, mustard oil, lemon juice, tomato paste, wine vinegar, and spices. Fear not—it's not as scorching as Dave's Insanity (see page 115), and makes a fantastic hot cocktail sauce.

Desert Rose Tamarind Hot Sauce

Costa Rica

From a company in Tucson comes this luscious, well-rounded sauce, with a ripe, fruity flavor from the tamarind, papayas, and bananas, a tart reminder from the pineapple vinegar, and a whiff of heat at the finish from the aged habanero mash and fresh cayenne peppers. One California retailer notifies its customers of a new shipment of Desert Rose by placing a single rose bud in its shop window.

Eslat Wheat Germ Hot Sauce

Trinidad

That's wheat germ floating in this sauce. Also habaneros, garlic, vinegar, salt, sugar, and spices. In a nod to Trinidad's colonial heritage, the label proclaims the sauce has been made since 1880 "by gourmet experts appointed by royalty."

F.T. (no) Wimps

North Carolina

Fresh, citric, and tart, this sauce has an up-front heat from the jalapeños and back-up flavor from fresh lime juice, onions, and garlic. Rick Brooks grew up in Michigan, where the only seasoning his mother used was salt and pepper ("and light on the pepper"). As a silver-smith he moved to Arizona to study with the Navajos, where he fell in love with jalapeños and spicy foods. He lives in North Carolina now, where he's a goldsmith by day and a hot sauce maker by night.

Firemist Spray Hot Sauce

Florida

Squeaky clean and crisp, this straightforward sauce blends cayenne peppers and paprika with black pepper, vinegar, and salt. It comes in several heat levels in a tidy spray bottle. "While eating eggs one morning it occurred to me that there had to be a better way to apply hot sauce instead of a drop here and a splash there," explained creator Michael Erickson. "Why not mist them?" Indeed.

Flaming Yellow Canary

North Carolina

From the maker of F.T. (no) Wimps, this sauce has banana peppers, vinegar, fresh-squeezed citrus, garlic, and sea salt. A percentage of the profits go to hearing-impaired children.

Flying Burrito Flounder Juice

North Carolina

Carolina sweet potatoes are featured in this driving blend of habaneros, Barbados molasses, garlic juice, and apple cider vinegar. The sweet taste of the South is almost immediately eclipsed by the escalating heat of the habaneros, which make this sauce "right hot!," as maker Phil Campbell says. As chef/owner of the Flying Burrito restaurant in Chapel Hill, he found sweet potatoes to be a perfect sweet foil to the heat. He spends part of each year in Quintana Roo, Mexico, "researching" Mayan cuisine. The first food he tried the sauce on was flounder, hence the name.

Hawaiian Passion Lilikoi Hot Sauce

🌶️🌶️🌶️   *Hawaii*

A bright, fragrant taste, made with lilikoi (passion fruit) juice, vinegar, and Thai bird and Hawaiian chiles. Not shown is **Hawaiian Passion Fire Sauce** (🌶️🌶️🌶️), a mouth-puckering blend of fresh Hawaiian ginger root, cider vinegar, and Thai bird and Hawaiian chiles.

Hawaiian Passion Pineapple Pepper Sauce

🌶️   *Hawaii*

Made originally at the request of Dole, this is a thin, fruity sauce featuring pineapple juice, along with Thai bird and Hawaiian chiles. One customer uses it on ice cream, and claims withdrawal symptoms when his supply runs out.

Heat

🌶️🌶️🌶️ 🌿   *North Carolina*

Can anyone guess the sixteen peppers in this dark, woody, almost bitter sauce? New Mexico red, cayenne, tabasco, jalapeño, cowhorn, habanero, pasilla negro, mirasol guajillo, arbol, and japone chiles (leaving six to guess) are blended with vinegar, onions, garlic, and sea salt. Great with grilled meats.

Hoot Mon Hot Mustard

North Carolina

A spicy, mustard-based sauce enhanced with honey, Scotch bonnet peppers, ginger, turmeric, and other spices, made by the Clevenger family (see page 22).

Iguana Red Pepper Sauce

Costa Rica

A light, subtle blend of cayenne peppers, carrots, tomato paste, and molasses. Imported and labeled by Half Moon Bay Trading Company, the sauce is made in Costa Rica, where it's popular, I'm told, on barbecued iguana.

Kayak Jack's Survival Sauce

Maine

Dense and textured, this complex sauce is ripe with the flavors of roasted sweet peppers and plum tomatoes, which are framed by fresh French tarragon and a roasted garlic purée. A hint of heat is provided by roasted red jalapeños. It's made on Vinalhaven, an island off the coast of Maine, by a man who wanted to make a fat-free lobster sauce, but quickly realized that the broad flavors went beyond seafood. A portion of the proceeds go to Hurricane Island Outward Bound.

Liquid Sky

🌶🌶🌶🌶 *Massachusetts*

Jimmy Fahey serves great barbecue at a neighborhood sports bar in Cambridge. Even from the street you can smell the pit barbecue, basted generously with Liquid Sky, which will send you soaring. "I could buy pure capsaicin and murder you," he quips, "but it's just tongue drano. I'm after flavor." It's a smoky, gutsy blend of habaneros and chipotles, filled in with ketchup, Worcestershire sauce, pure black molasses, and liquid smoke.

Mad Dog Liquid Fire Hot Sauce

🌶🌶🌶🌿 *Massachusetts*

Laced with African bird's eye peppers, jalapeños, and concentrated pepper extract, this sauce is balanced with spices, unsulphured molasses, and tomato paste.

Mancha's Original Wimp Sauce

🌶 *Alabama*

From Mancha's Restaurant (see page 98) comes an earthy, mild sauce with vegetables, spices, vinegar, and a floral suggestion of habaneros.

Mosquito Coast Dead Men Tell No Tales

🌶🌶🌶🌿 *Florida*

A rustic blend of tomatoes, habaneros, vinegar, herbs, and spices from Tampa Bay.

Mother's Mountain Fire Eater Hot Pepper Sauce

Maine

A frankly mustard sauce made intriguing by the addition of tamari sauce and rum, with sneaky heat from the cayenne and New Mexico red peppers.

Mr. Spice Tangy Bang Hot Sauce

Rhode Island

A subtle concoction of ginger, honey, horseradish, lime juice, garlic juice, onion juice, apple cider vinegar, and cayenne and ciquomi rokete peppers.

Mrs. Dog's Dangerously Hot Pepper Sauce

Michigan

With a supple texture and persistent heat, this clean sauce is made with Portuguese and habanero peppers, allspice, vinegar, and salt. The company is named after Julie Applegate's pet, Mrs. Dog. Inspiration for the whimsical product names (Mrs. Dog's Disappearing Mustard Sauce, Dangerously Hot Pepper Sauce) came from her childhood fascination with her grandmother's Elizabeth Arden cosmetics, which have such names as Eight Hour Cream, Especially Gentle Shampoo, and Visible Difference. (Not one to be catty, Julie sells her items in a mail-order dogalog.)

Muirhead Dragon's Breath Sherry Pepper Sauce

New Jersey

From a restaurant in New Jersey comes this sauce that greets you with a jolt of sherry, cut ever so slightly by tomato sauce, followed by an herb-habanero finish. Not shown is **Muirhead Dragon's Breath Habanero Sauce** (), a tongue-tingling sherry spiked with habaneros and herbs.

No Joke Hot Sauce

Washington

Ripe with tomatoes, which are immediately eclipsed by the ricocheting heat of habaneros, serranos, chipotles, and jalapenos, this chunky sauce is bolstered with vinegar and salt. Insistently hot (no joke), this is one of many hot sauces that evolved in a small family restaurant, in this case Zavala's Place in Othello, Washington. **No Joke for Beginners Hot Sauce** () is a mild stew of tomatoes, jalapeños, vinegar, and salt.

Oak Hill Farms Vidalia Onion Hot Sauce

Georgia

From an Atlanta-based company specializing in southern recipes, best known to hot sauce fans for Scorned Woman (see page 93), comes this deep, beautifully balanced sauce with a hint of sweetness from the famous Georgia onions, plus tabasco peppers, vinegar, and salt. They also make **Oak Hill Farms Herb & Garlic Hot Sauce** (), which is spicy and peppery, with tabasco peppers, vinegar, garlic, herbs, and spices; and **Oak Hill Farms Three Pepper Lemon Hot Sauce** (), an aromatic blend of tabasco and green chiles, vinegar, and lemon juice, deeply flecked with black pepper. (Three Pepper Lemon sauce is identical to Scorned Woman hot sauce, minus the habaneros.)

Pepper Creek Farms Jalapeño TNT

Oklahoma

With a fresh, herbal nose, this jalapeño-based sauce incorporates fresh horseradish and garlic with apple cider vinegar. From an Oklahoma company that's been producing spicy condiments since 1984.

Pepper Plant Hot Pepper Sauce Original California Style

California

A thick, ebony-colored sauce of peppers, garlic, onions, olive oil, vinegar, and spices. Not shown are **Pepper Plant Hot Pepper Sauce with Garlic** ( ), which is similar but has a lot of fresh garlic; and **Pepper Plant Chipotle Sauce with Smoked Jalapeño** ( ), a thick, somewhat sweet sauce of molasses, jalapeños, onions, carrots, garlic, vinegar, smoke flavoring, and olive oil. Pepper Plant sauces are made by friends and pepper lovers, Bob Roush and Irv Silveira. Both have day jobs, and grind their peppers at night.

Ralph's Sweet Hot Sauce

New York

This thick mahogany spread of pure cane sugar, lemon juice, and wine vinegar is startled by the biting heat of red Thai and habanero chiles. Made in Ithaca by a southerner raised in a household where "hot peppers were grown like roses around the yard."

Rebel Fire No. 1 Jalapeño Hot Sauce

 *Ontario*

Beautifully balanced and packed with flavor, this Canadian sauce is a gourmet version of a Mexican salsa. It's a stylish blend of fresh tomatoes, jalapeños, celery, bell peppers, and fresh garlic, highlighted by the earthy aroma of cumin, Mexican oregano, and coriander. With no salt or sugar, it's from a Welshman and an Arkansas native, who teamed up in Toronto.

Rehoboth Beach Boardwalk Vidalia Onion & Georgia Peach Hot Sauce

Delaware

A supple, sweet, somewhat thickish sauce, featuring Georgia onions and peaches, onions, spices, and a hint of chiles. The peaches work.

River Run Hot Sauce

 *Vermont*

Emboldened with habaneros, jalapeños, and fresno chiles, this pumpkin-colored sauce is refined with rice wine vinegar, shallots, olive oil, garlic, and salt. With a beautiful consistency and smooth texture, this sauce was a collaborative effort of the owners and customers of the River Run Restaurant in tiny Plainfield, Vermont, known for its food and extensive hot sauce collection. The man behind it is owner/chef Jimmy Kennedy (a longtime partner in New York's Acme Bar and Grill), a Mississippian who likes to serve southern food with a seasoned twist.

Rowena's Red Lightning Hot Sauce

Virginia

Three fruit trees in the backyard led Rowena Fullinwider to make jams and jellies in 1983. She now has eighteen employees and makes authentic period dry mixes for Colonial Williamsburg, as well as this light, herbal sauce with a generous streak of tomatoes, blended with cayenne peppers, onions, garlic, dry mustard, vinegar, and spices.

Scorned Woman Hot Sauce

Georgia

She comes in a black bag and hath fury. Habaneros, green chiles, and tabasco peppers are tempered slightly in a pourable blend of vinegar, lemon juice, and loads of black pepper.

Try Me Dragon Sauce

Louisiana

With a soy sauce base, this mild sauce with a spicy finish is found in supermarkets nationwide, one in a line of Try Me sauces from Reily Foods in Louisiana (see page 46).

Try Me Tiger Sauce

Louisiana

Sweet, sour, and spicy, this mild sauce made with a cayenne pepper mash isn't called a "hot" sauce intentionally—it's Tiger Sauce—and people consider it their own personal discovery, a "secret ingredient" for ribs, pork, and chicken. With twenty-eight ingredients, this sauce has been on the market for thirty-five years and commands ardent fans—such as the boy who claimed he made his mother drive 200 miles to keep Tiger in his tank.

Vampfire Hot Sauce

Louisiana

Seeing the booming popularity of habanero hot sauces (which have grown to 10 percent of the market in the last few years), many Louisiana hot sauce makers are introducing habanero hot sauces. Made by Panola (see page 41) with habanero, tabasco, and cayenne peppers, plus spices and lemon oil.

Vic's Original Fire Sauce

Nevada

One drop at a time is enough of this piercingly hot sauce of vinegar, peppers, garlic, and salt.

The Wizard's Habanero Super Hot Stuff

California

Organic ingredients are found in this medium-hot sauce of habanero and cayenne pepper mash, honey, umeboshi vinegar, organic red miso, natural herbs, and spices. **The Wizard's Original Hot Stuff** ( ) is similar in flavor, but milder, and also with umeboshi plums, apple fiber, and natural seaweed extract.

Death and Destruction

While some labels speak to the fervor that hot sauce inspires (Jump Up and Kiss Me, Inner Beauty), others challenge us to try a sauce that would kill mere mortals—with names and imagery ranging from nuclear explosions to Catholic last rites. This macho tradition has ancient roots: according to ancient Cora Indian mythology, when the first man leaped onto the banquet table of life, his testicles turned to chiles, and by dancing he shook the pungent seeds onto everyone's food, which they apparently enjoyed.

Blair's Death Sauce

New Jersey

From a bar in New Jersey comes this combustible sauce, which blends habaneros and chipotles with lime juice, vinegar, cilantro, and other fresh herbs. "I've always had a taste for hot food," said co-creator Blair Lazar, who, like many hot sauce makers, started bottling the sauce in his restaurant kitchen and serving it to intrepid diners. "You either love it or you don't."

Firehouse Global Warming Tamarind Chipotle Sauce

Colorado

From the chef at the Firehouse Bar and Grill in Denver, this versatile tamarind-based chipotle sauce is a beautiful mahogany brown, with a nice smoky taste, subtle burn, and rich flavor from the blending of tomatoes, tamarind, onions, and spices.

Gib's Nuclear Hell Hot Pepper Sauce

Kentucky

From Gib's Smoke House & Grill in Louisville (where meats are basted in this sauce then smoked for hours in the big smoker out back), comes this sauce that's almost as thick as the main ingredient of tomato paste, plus spices and plenty of jalapeños that provide a lingering, back-of-the-throat explosive heat.

Habanero Hot Sauce With A Half Life

 New York

In 1973, upstate New Yorker Bill Richer went west, taking with him a love for Buffalo wings. In Arizona, friends introduced him to the habanero, which he crafted into a sauce "with a taste of Armageddon in every drop." When Richer returned to Amherst, New York, he began bottling the sauce in the kitchen of the place where he tended bar. To keep up with growing demand, Richer now bottles his sauce in Jacksonville, Florida. In the Louisiana style, this salty sauce has habanero and Scotch bonnet peppers, vinegar, onions, and salt.

Last Rites

Pennsylvania

With some of the funniest labels on the market (see Capital Punishment, page 108), Kenny and Wendy Roda of Hot Heads have the good humor, outrageousness, and passion for hot foods that is the hallmark of this business. Who would think of designing a label with a bow-tied chile pepper in a coffin? "This sauce will make even a priest go to confession," they proclaim, "and it might make an attorney tell the truth." A former road musician, platinum trader, and runaway youth counselor, Kenny now serves with Wendy as a tour escort in the Yucatan Peninsula. For several months, they live in a Mayan village, where their Mayan housekeeper takes them to other villages on Sundays to eat with families. "We started watching Indians cook achiote, habaneros, jalapeños, and bay leaves on stone-made stoves on the floor with a good-smelling wood, and were hit by the aroma." Part-time spice traders, they returned home to Lancaster, Pennsylvania, and started making sauces. This thick, spicy sauce is loaded with Scotch bonnet peppers, vinegar, allspice, and natural spices.

Mancha's Original Agent Orange Sauce

Alabama

From a restaurant in Alabama comes this sauce (simply a mash of habaneros and vinegar) that's hot and floral. At the age of thirteen, Rebecca Mancha's grandfather-in-law walked north from Chihuahua, Mexico. He got tired of walking in Birmingham, and made his home there. With one arm and limited English, the one thing he knew how to do was make hot tamales—which he sold from a pushcart on the streets of Birmingham in the 1920s. He eventually opened Mancha's Restaurant. Fifteen years ago, friends of Rebecca and her husband brought back two habaneros from Belize. Rebecca's husband, who was eating a sandwich with aluminum foil around it, popped the pepper into his mouth while eating the sandwich. "He mowed through that sandwich, foil and all," Rebecca recalled. "It was the hottest thing he'd ever tasted." Rebecca's husband held up the remaining pepper, and told his wife that this little pepper would make them famous. They started growing habaneros and making sauces. (Demand now causes Rebecca to have them grown organically on a nearby farm.) A customer named the sauce Agent Orange.

Mancha's Original Nuclear Sauce

Alabama

From Mancha's Restaurant in Birmingham, a thick, green mash of fresh jalapeños, vinegar, and spices.

Red Dog Tavern Nuclear Waste Sauce

New York

From a bar in the Adirondacks (see page 116) comes this combustible sauce. Made by a former navy sea dog who hopes the sauce will fill out his retirement, Nuclear Waste is made in the kitchen out back by grinding up habaneros, adding just enough honey to dull the pain, and blending it with a Vietnamese garlic chile paste.

Trauma Super Hot Sauce

🌶️🌶️🌶️🌶️   *New Jersey*

Made with pepper extract, garlic, vinegar, salt, and spices, this bitter sauce is almost pure heat. From Sim Baron, who also makes the lively Ieeowch!!! (see page 112).

Virgin Islands Apocalyptic Hot Sauce

🌶️🌶️🌶️🌶️ 🌿   *St. Thomas*

A smooth blend of just habaneros and vinegar. The taste of fresh peppers is overwhelming in this Caribbean-style sauce.

Religious Experiences

Inevitably, hot sauce imagery conjures up religious experiences, from heavenly ingredients to hellish tastes. Fortunately, both God and the Devil love hot sauce—it's limbo you have to worry about.

Dan T's Inferno Mustard Cayenne Sauce

 Ontario

When Dan Taylor went to print his beautiful labels, the printer balked until he had discussed the art with his church elders, not wanting to commit blasphemy. The church put his mind to rest, as the hellfire and damnation theme was a concept with which they were already working. Alluding to the first book of the 13th-century poem describing the Italian poet's allegoric descent into hell, Dan T's line features ceramic-coated bottles, superb artwork, and richly flavored sauces. He claims these are sauces from down under... "and we don't mean Australia!" This light orange cayenne sauce is infused with tomato paste, lemon juice, mustard flour, and spices.

Dan T's Inferno Whitehot Cayenne Sauce

Ontario

Those who like Louisiana hot sauces but find them not hot enough will enjoy this cayenne pepper sauce that is thickened and flavored with tomato paste, lemon juice, and spices, and enflamed with red pepper extract. "It appeals to hot sauce aficionados," says Dan T., "and it's great for stripping furniture. "He also makes **Dan T's Inferno Spiced Cayenne Sauce** ( ) with cayenne peppers, tomato paste, lemon juice, white vinegar, and spices.

Dinosaur's Devils Duel Fiendishly Hot Habañero Pepper Sauce

New York

From a biker bar with great barbecue and live blues. Mike Rotella and John Stage started in 1983 with a 55-gallon drum cut in half, selling barbecue at biker shows up and down the East Coast. In 1988, they opened the Dinosaur Bar-B-Q in Syracuse, which attracts amazing music acts. They make this sauce with fresh habaneros, onions, green peppers, celery, mustard, garlic, and spices. (They also make a Wango Tango barbecue sauce.) How'd they get the name Dinosaur? In 1983, the music scene was "just terrible," according to Stage. "We were still listening to the Allman Brothers and I was riding a '57 Panhead. We were dinosaurs."

Firehouse Satan's Slow Burn Smoky Habanero Hot Sauce

Colorado

The chef at the Firehouse Bar & Grill in Denver makes a terrific smoked habanero salsa, and their bottled sauces are imaginative and extremely flavorful. With smoked habaneros this sauce has a slow burn that sneaks up on you but doesn't overpower the tomatoes, tomatillos, garlic, onions, vinegar, and spices that give it a great base.

Habañero Hot Sauce from Hell

Arizona

A husband and wife team in Phoenix makes this and a line of southwestern hot sauces that are distinguished by their strong flavors and imaginative packaging. With habaneros, fresh carrots, garlic, vinegar, and spices, this sauce is hot and flavorful. Unfortunately, plastic resins have become so expensive that they are discontinuing the melting red wax on the bottle. (If you have one, save this collector's item!)

Halfway to Pure Hell Hot Sauce

Colorado

How can one resist this label? With a mild dose of habanero and pequin peppers, this sauce is versatile and slightly sweet, with pineapple juice, brown sugar, honey, and spices.

Hell in a Bottle Hot Sauce

California

He's known as Chili Bill Eichinger ("don't call me *Mr.* Chili—it sounds like a hairdresser"), and one of the many features that distinguishes this charming man is that he's tattooed from head to foot, mostly with chiles (one tattoo features a skull with chiles emerging from the mouth). His thick, flavorful sauce is also distinguished by applesauce, which Chili Bill blends deftly with onions, habaneros, garlic, and lime juice. Like many sauce makers, he cares about quality and is "a working stiff" with two jobs to keep the sauce coming. He got into hot foods in the 1970s doing chili cookoffs (hence his nickname), but doesn't compete anymore—"the politics and glamor of it all sorta did me in."

Hellfire & Damnation

Costa Rica

From the incorrigible Park Kerr at the El Paso Chile Company comes this sauce with habaneros, thick with fresh carrots and onions, and flavored with garlic, lime juice, vinegar, and lots of salt.

Holy City Heat

South Carolina

Hailing from coastal South Carolina, this mild, tasty sauce is made with the Charleston hot pepper, a cayenne hybrid with the light citrus tones of the habanero, developed by the U.S. Department of Agriculture. "In Charleston in the summertime," sauce maker Mike Zemke explained, "you don't get hot, you are hot, and you stay that way. Humidity during the summer stays close to the 100 percent mark. But the climate is ideal for growing capsicums." The pepper is tempered with the sweet overtones of pineapple juice and sweet potatoes. It's made by the folks who produce Bubba (see page 80) barbecue sauces and condiments.

Holy Habañero!

🌶 🌶 🌶 🌶 🌿

Pennsylvania

From the Brown Adobe, a small company that makes food products by hand, comes this chunky southwestern-style, tomato-based sauce with habaneros and New Mexico red chiles, onions, vinegar, garlic, and spices.

Hot as Hell

🌶 🌶 🌶 🌶 🌿

New Jersey

This concentrated sauce is a sambal, commonly used in Chinese, Indian, and Indonesian dishes. It was developed by Nick ten Velde, an Indonesian who spent his teenage years in a Japanese concentration camp. As a woodcutter in the camps, he would go into the jungle, where he'd gather Spanish chiles and trade them secretly within the camps. (The prisoners would burn their mouths with the chiles so that they could eat the food.) He later moved to the Netherlands, and then the United States, and started making a line of all-natural Indonesian sambals (see page 69) that show the influence of many foreign cultures—Indian, Chinese, Arabian, and Dutch colonial.

Hot Stuff Jab Jab

🌶 🌶 🌶 🌶

Trinidad

Jab-jab is Trinidadian slang for the devil, chanted during Carnival to call him out. Of the Caribbean style, the sauce is imported by David Jenkins, who started New York's first hot food store in Greenwich Village (which, sadly, has closed), but still operates a mail-order business called Hot Stuff. The sauce is blended with habaneros, papayas, lime, garlic, and tropical spices. Papaya is a natural meat tenderizer, and so this sauce is a great marinade.

Montezuma Devil's Tingle Hot Sauce

🌶🌶🍃   *Ohio*

You'll find *salsa endiablada* (deviled sauce) in markets of the central Mexican valley. From Montezuma (see page 60), this Oaxacan recipe features the pasilla negro (black raisin) chile, vinegar, corn oil, garlic, herbs, and spices, in a light, earthy, vinegary sauce.

Mother's Mountain Habanero Heaven Deadly Pepper Sauce

🌶🌶🌶🍃   *Maine*

A smooth, clean sauce of habaneros, tomato paste, mustard, and natural spice extract, made in southern Maine since 1989 by a woman who loves spicy foods.

Pure Hell Hot Sauce

🌶🌶🌶🌶   *Colorado*

With habaneros and crushed red peppers, this sauce is similar to Halfway to Pure Hell (see page 102), but scorchingly hotter.

Religious Experience

🌶️🌶️🌶️ 🌿   *Colorado*

From a former Montana river guide, this sauce might technically be classified as a salsa, but Jeff McFadden "just couldn't stand that whole salsa and Santa Fe thing." Unusual in the industry, he uses fresh tomatoes, as well as a variety of chiles (jalapeño, pequín, and African cayenne), fresh tomatillos, cilantro, and spices. The sauce is aromatic and fresh, with a strong tomatillo flavor and a beautiful texture. Like many sauce makers, he struggled for four years, and now can't make the sauce fast enough. People leave late-night calls on his machine telling of their "religious experiences," a former nun sends him her vegetable poetry, and the manager of an oil and battery store in Wombat, Australia, wrote asking to be made head of distribution on the continent.

Road to Hell Hot Sauce

🌶️🌶️🌶️   *Colorado*

From Eric Walton, a Denver chef who has long seen the link between bikers and hot foods, comes this thick, beautiful sauce of habaneros and red peppers, plus tomato juice, garlic, carrots, and spices. "It's like standing barefoot on a desert road at noon," says Eric, who also makes Pure Hell (see page 105) and Halfway to Pure Hell (see page 102).

Satan's Revenge Chili Sauce

🌶️🌶️🌶️🌶️ 🌿   *New Jersey*

From Cosmopolitan Foods comes this oily, salt-free, excruciatingly hot sauce that is a mixture of imported Chinese, Indian, and Indonesian chiles, onions, lemon juice, unsaturated vegetable oil, garlic, and spices. The label warns that it will "get you in the end." Nick ten Velde also makes a dried spice blend called "I Am on Fire, Ready to Die!"

Politically Incorrects

In no other corner of the food world will you find such outrageous names and labels. While some find the more daring labels offensive, sexist, and the like, there's no doubt that they push the edge, giving our thoughts as much of a leap as our taste buds.

Capital Punishment

                    Pennsylvania

Sporting a chile pepper in the electric chair, the label claims that this sauce was created for those who treat every meal as if it were their last. "Once the bottle is opened, not even a call from the governor can save you." Not only is Capital Punishment legal in all fifty states, but it's being sold to the California penal system. (The crack up is that they insist on buying the sauce without labels.) An electric blend of hot chiles (tepin, serrano, African mombasa, habanero), vinegar, onions, herbs, and spices.

Hot Bitch at the Beach

Delaware

From Chip Hearn, owner of the Starboard Restaurant (see page 36), comes this blend of sweet potatoes, ginger purée, garlic juice, Barbados molasses, clear shoyu (a light, sweet soy sauce made with wheat and soy bean that serves as a natural stabilizer), key lime juice, and spices, with a hot, lasting finish from Mexican habaneros and cayenne mash.

Hot Buns at the Beach

Delaware

Just so you won't think he's sexist, here's Chip Hearn's counterpart to Hot Bitch, identical except that this sauce has less ginger and a third pepper: the rica red (a hybrid habanero from Costa Rica).

Hot Ketchita

 Mexico

From Hot Heads of Pennsylvania (see page 97), this "hot tomato" is a purée of tomatoes, habaneros, vinegar, salt, and spices.

Mild Ketchita

 Mexico

The same ingredients as Hot Kechita (above), but milder.

Hot Mama's Gourmet Hickory Smoked Jalapeño Sauce

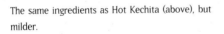 *Arizona*

The hickory smell and aroma are evident in this green jalapeño sauce with onions, cider vinegar, salt, and fresh garlic.

Mean Devil Woman Cajun Pepper Sauce

Michigan

Tart and spicy, this tomato-based sauce of Chinese red and habanero peppers, vinegar, vegetable oil, garlic, white pepper and lime juice is made by a guy named Cajun Radar, who cooks at a restaurant in Gretna, Louisiana, and teamed up with a dentist-turned-real estate auctioneer-turned-sauce distributor from Kalamazoo, who loves the sauce.

Panola 10 Point Hot Sauce

 *Louisiana*

Hunters will deerly appreciate this mild sauce in a camouflage green plastic bottle (with a Day-Glo orange cap!) to take into the woods. A mixture of cayenne and jalapeño peppers, vinegar, onions, sugar, salt, and spices, from Panola Pepper Corporation (see page 41).

Spicy Chesapeake Seafood Hot Sauce

Delaware

From the folks who brought you Hot Bitch and Hot Buns (see page 108), here's a spicy mustard sauce with white wine vinegar, tabasco peppers, horseradish, and lemon juice.

Ultimate Burn

Delaware

Chip Hearn was talking with his father about a beer promotion at the Starboard Restaurant when he recalled a Mexican beer bottle with a scratch-off label. "I stopped in mid-sentence," he recalled, "and ran to the phone to call my printer." He applied the technique to this label, which adorns an all-natural sturdy sauce with a range of flavors—everything from sweet potatoes to mango purée, ginger purée, and lime juice, highlighted by a clear habanero heat and lip-smacking cayenne finish. She comes clothed, but you can scratch off the bikini top.

Screamers

These labels and names so elegantly express my first
experience with hot sauce that they belong in a cat-
egory by themselves.

Coyote Cocina Howlin' Hot Sauce

🌶️🌶️🌶️🌶️ *Jamaica*

A Caribbean-style sauce made by southwestern guru Mark Miller, of the acclaimed Coyote Cafe in Santa Fe. A clean, floral sauce of Scotch bonnet peppers, vinegar, and spices.

Craig's HOT! Pepper Sauce

🌶️🌶️🌶️🌿 *New Jersey*

Strong and herbal, this thick, earthy sauce clamps down on the palate with a medley of peppers (habaneros and jalapeños primarily, but also cayenne and cherry peppers), swirled with tomatoes, vinegar, and herbs. It's made by Craig Neivert, a Wall Street broker, and his wife Cindy, who are proud to represent the Garden State (as the label says, "it's New Jersey's Finest"). I love the *Mad Magazine*-inspired label, which is hand colored.

Ieeowch!!! Hot Sauce

🌶️🌶️🌶️🌶️ *New Jersey*

The label says it all in this sauce of African bird's eye peppers, water, vinegar, garlic, and spices from Sim Baron, a caterer in New Jersey with a background in scientific engineering. Sim was looking for a low-sodium sauce that could replace the Louisiana-style sauces, which he found overpowering and intrusive. It is the first hot sauce sold in the United States in a medicine dropper bottle.

Pain Is Good

🌶️🌶️🌶️🌶️🌿 *Kansas*

This torrid sauce is assertive with habaneros, backed up by carrots, lemon and lime juice, olive oil, vinegar, and mustard. "There is a point where pleasure and pain intersect," claim the makers. "A doorway to a new dimension of sensual euphoria. Where fire both burns and soothes. Where heat engulfs every neuron within you. Once the line is crossed, once the bottle is opened, once it touches your lips, there is no going back. Pain is good." They also make Besos de Fuego (see page 81).

Screaming Sphincter Hot Sauce

🌶️🌶️🌶️   *Texas*

This hot sauce was delivered to my back door with a corn cob (as if the label didn't speak for itself.) What can you say about a company whose tag line is "a burning painus within the anus"? With the consistency of a thinnish salsa, this tomato-based sauce has carrots, garlic, sesame oil, and onions, as well as pequín peppers that provide a hot finish.

Texas Tears Habanero Pepper Sauce

🌶️🌶️🌶️🌶️🌿   *Texas*

A vibrant, bracing habanero sauce that is refined and sweetened ever so slightly by the fresh carrots, onions, garlic, and lime juice. Concocted by J. P. Hayes for the Austin Hot Sauce Contest, it's become a local favorite, and was changed from Texas Tears to Tejas Tears (original label shown). Try it in gumbos, soups, and salad dressings.

Tongues of Fire The Unspeakable Hot Sauce

🌶️🌶️🌶️🌶️   *Illinois*

The floral heat of habaneros is evident in this unadulterated, pretty orange Jamaican-style sauce of simply Scotch bonnets, vinegar, salt, and onions.

The Untouchables

Everyone has a friend (or enemy) for whom "nothing is too hot," someone they want to impress, surprise, or kill. The following sauces have a pepper extract made by shooting hexane through a pepper mash and extracting the capsaicin. Capsaicin is clumpy (and deadly—the FDA won't allow you to possess without a permit), so chemists add oil to dilute it into an extract. It's long been used in pepper spray, but an enterprising—some say crazy—guy named Dave added it to hot sauce in 1991, and the hot sauce world hasn't been the same.

Blair's After Death Sauce

🌶 🌶 🌶 🌶 🌶

New Jersey

From a restaurant in New Jersey, this piercingly hot sauce doesn't reach the shock level of Dave's (below), but is still deadly. The sauce has a medley of peppers (habaneros, cayenne, chipotle), lime juice, cilantro, and herbs, which are all but eclipsed by the pepper extract.

Dave's Insanity Sauce

🌶 🌶 🌶 🌶 🌶

California

Dave's Insanity is so hot that it was banned from the Fiery Foods Show after a guy started hyperventilating and organizers had to call 911. A former restaurateur, Dave—who attends food shows in a straitjacket—vowed to make the world's hottest sauce ("mostly to shut up the drunks at the bar late at night"). He added capsaicin extract to his sauce and tested it at the restaurant, where customers kept telling him he was insane. Believe it or not, the #1 ingredient in Dave's Insanity is tomato sauce, which he combines with Indian and Asian habaneros, anaheims, jalapeños, and extract. One writer quipped that "Dave's is to regular hot sauce what grain alcohol is to beer—good stuff to serve your ex-spouse or guests who have worn out their welcome." Dave is good-natured about all this, and says one drop will add zing to any dish. (He also claims his sauce is not as hot as the red savina, a habanero pepper with 326,000 Scoville units.)

Dave's Insanity Private Reserve, Limited Edition

🌶 🌶 🌶 🌶 🌶

California

Just when you thought it couldn't get any hotter, Dave made a private reserve sauce that is twice as hot as Insanity (measuring 320,000 scoville units). Made once a year, bottles are hand-signed and dated, and wrapped in a coffin—er, crate—sealed with yellow CAUTION tape. With tomato sauce, onions, red savinas, vinegar, spices, soy oil, garlic, salt, and twice the extract.

Endorphin Rush
Beyond Hot Sauce

🌶️🌶️🌶️🌶️🌶️

Illinois

Capsaicin—the chemical that gives peppers their heat—is said to trigger endorphins, creating a pleasurable rush similar to a jogger's high. Thick, dense, and dark, this sauce has a momentary flicker of sweetness from the molasses, which is swallowed up by the exhausting heat. Also with tomato paste and soy sauce.

Mad Dog Inferno Hot Sauce

🌶️🌶️🌶️🌶️🌶️

Massachusetts

At chile festivals, David Ashley proffers samples of this tastebud-obliterating sauce with a toothpick. There's a moment of flavor from the garlic, onions, clove, and unsulphured molasses, engulfed almost immediately in the pain of the concentrated pepper extract.

Red Dog Tavern
Armageddon Sauce

🌶️🌶️🌶️🌶️🌶️

New York

The Red Dog Tavern is a bar in the Adirondack Mountains of upstate New York where summer camp counselors from Buffalo kept teasing former navy sea dog Ted Klamm about making his chicken wing sauce hotter. To shut them up he made Armageddon, which is mouth-shatteringly hot. (Ted, by the way, makes his own extract, squeezing red savina habaneros in a food processor then juicer to extract the oil.) If you can eat a dozen wings marinated in Armageddon, he'll put your name on the wall at the bar (behind the live tarantula). In five years, only fifteen have succeeded (and yours truly wasn't one of them). (By the way, Ted claims there is tomato paste and sriracha sauce in the bottle, but I couldn't get past the heat.) He also makes Nuclear Waste (see page 98).

RECIPES

Chipotle Red Sauce for Grilled Meat or Fish

The flavor and textures of this sauce are reminiscent of the moles and pipians (sauces made from ground nuts and seeds) of Mexico. Enjoy this sauce on eggs or sandwiches, add a dollop to your favorite soup, or simply scoop it up in a fresh warm tortilla.

4 cloves garlic
Olive oil
2 ancho chiles
1/2 cup sliced almonds
1/8 cup sesame seeds
2 tablespoons diced white onion
1 teaspoon salt
2 tablespoons chipotle hot sauce
1/2 cup chicken stock

Preheat oven to 400°. Rub garlic cloves with olive oil, place on cookie sheet, and roast until brown all over, stirring occasionally, about 5 minutes. Meanwhile, place ancho chiles in hot water for 20 minutes to reconstitute, then drain and finely chop. Remove garlic from oven, and when cooled, squeeze garlic from peel. Place almonds and sesame seeds into a food processor and purée. Add chiles, onion, garlic, salt, and hot sauce and purée to combine. With machine running, add the chicken stock slowly and blend until well combined.

Makes 1 cup

Habanero Hot Sauce

Hot sauces with habanero chiles are the staple seasoning
of the Caribbean. They can be as simple as chiles and vinegar, or embellished with various vegetables (carrots, onions,
pumpkin), and/or fruits (papayas, passion fruit, mangos).

> 1 fresh habanero, stemmed
> 2 carrots
> 1 medium onion
> 1 cup distilled white vinegar
> 2 cloves garlic
> Juice of 1 lime

Purée ingredients in blender. Pour into saucepan and bring
to a boil. Simmer for a few minutes, then remove from heat.
Let cool, and pour into sterilized containers.

Makes 2 cups

Sangre de Diablo Sauce

This "blood of the devil" sauce is fiery, and great over
grilled shrimp or tossed with a red pepper pasta. Top with
some crumbled feta cheese and serve with Dos Equis beer.
This sauce is also very tasty strained and served as a
bottled condiment.

> 2 tablespoons olive oil
> 1 cup diced yellow onion
> 1 green bell pepper, diced
> 6 cloves garlic, minced
> 2 jalapeños, finely chopped
> 1 28-ounce can crushed tomatoes in purée
> 1 1/2 teaspoons salt
> 1 tablespoon red pepper flakes
> 1/2 cup red wine
> 1/4 cup habanero hot sauce with a slight
>   vinegar kick

Over medium-high heat, heat oil and sauté onion and pepper until they begin to soften. Add garlic, stir for a moment,
then add jalapeños, tomatoes, salt, pepper flakes, and red
wine and simmer for 20 minutes. Add 1/8 cup hot sauce,
stir, taste, and add up to 1/8 cup more hot sauce if desired.
Stir again and remove from heat.

Makes 5 cups

Bandana's Blues Barbecue Sauce

Great as a marinade or table dipping sauce. You can easily halve the recipe.

1/4 cup canola oil
1/4 cup brown sugar
1 cup diced Spanish onions
1 cup diced red onions
1/2 bunch scallions, finely diced
1 clove garlic, peeled and minced
3 blood oranges or regular oranges,
    peeled, seeded, and chopped
4 plum tomatoes (or 1/2-pound can),
    peeled and puréed
4 ounces tamarind sauce
1/4 cup Worcestershire sauce
1 cup tomato sauce
Juice of 1 1/2 lemons
1 cup orange juice, freshly squeezed
3 tablespoons mixed freshly ground
    black and white pepper
1/2 cup cumin seeds, toasted and ground
3/4 teaspoon fresh cayenne pepper
3 tablespoons Bandana's XXtra Serious Pepper Sauce
    or other fresh Caribbean habanero sauce

Heat the oil to smoking, add brown sugar, and stir constantly until it starts to thicken. Still stirring, add onions, scallions, and then garlic. Turn down heat, add oranges and tomato purée, and simmer 10 minutes. Add tamarind, Worcestershire, and tomato sauces, and lemon and orange juices, and reduce by one fourth, about 10 minutes. Add the black and white pepper, cumin, and cayenne pepper, and cook for 10 minutes over low to medium heat. Add hot sauce, and serve, or refrigerate for up to 2 weeks.

Makes 6 cups

Four-Pepper Papaya Salsa

Brightly flecked with red, yellow, and green, this salsa is a vibrant medley of color. Serve a dollop with grilled vegetables, fish, or chicken.

> 1 ripe mango, peeled
> 1 ripe papaya, peeled
> 1/2 red bell pepper, stemmed and seeded
> 1/2 yellow bell pepper, stemmed and seeded
> 1/2 green bell pepper, stemmed and seeded
> 1 serrano chile, stemmed and seeded
> 2 cloves garlic, minced
> 3 tablespoons lime juice, freshly squeezed
> 1 small red onion, finely chopped
> 1 1/2 teaspoons Caribbean habanero sauce

Combine mango, papaya, peppers, and chile in food processor and pulse lightly, taking care not to overblend. Combine with remaining ingredients in a bowl and mix well.

Makes 3 cups

Chilled Avocado Soup

You'll be surprised at how easy this lovely soup is to make and how light it is, despite the buttermilk and avocados.

> 2 cups buttermilk
> 2 cups avocado pulp (about 2 ripe avocados)
> 1 cucumber, peeled, seeded, and coarsely chopped
> 2 tablespoons diced white onion
> Zest and juice of 1 lime
> 1 teaspoon salt
> 1 teaspoon white pepper
> 2 cups milk
> 1 cup water
> 2 tablespoons Tabasco Jalapeño Sauce or another
>   smooth green hot sauce with a tangy finish
> Spicy Sour Cream (recipe follows)

Blend buttermilk and avocados in blender then add cucumber, onion, lime juice (reserving the zest), salt, and pepper. With blender running, add milk, water, and hot sauce. Chill and serve, garnished with a dollop of Spicy Sour Cream and a little lime zest.

Serves 8

Spicy Sour Cream

> 2 tablespoons El Yucateco green habanero sauce
>   or another smooth green hot sauce with a tangy
>   finish and a strong jolt of heat
> 1 tablespoon Tapatio or another smooth red
>   chile sauce
> 1 cup sour cream

Add hot sauces to the sour cream, and mix quickly with a fork so that the colors of the sauces streak the sour cream.

Makes 1 cup

Ratatouille

This adaptation of the rustic French vegetable dish adds a welcome zest to the wonderfully mellow taste of oven-roasted fall vegetables. Serve hot over a bed of couscous for a robust and colorful meal.

> 2 10-inch Japanese eggplants, sliced into 1/2-inch
>   rounds (about 4 cups)
> Kosher salt
> 2 cascabel chiles, or 1 teaspoon Mexican hot sauce
> 1/4 cup extra virgin olive oil
> 2 yellow onions, cut into bite-size wedges
> 2 cloves garlic, crushed
> 2 red bell peppers, cored, seeded, and cut
>   into eighths
> 2 green bell peppers, cored, seeded, and cut
>   into eighths
> 2 small zucchini, cut into 1/2-inch rounds
> 2 small yellow squash, cut into 1/2-inch rounds
> 1 (32-ounce) can Italian plum tomatoes, quartered,
>   with juice
> 2 teaspoons chipotle hot sauce
> 1 cup coarsely chopped Italian flat-leaf parsley
> 2 teaspoons crushed red pepper
> 2 teaspoons dried oregano

Place a layer of eggplant rounds in a large colander, sprinkle generously with kosher salt, and repeat until all rounds have been used. Allow to drain 1/2 hour or more, then rinse and dry thoroughly. Meanwhile, submerge cascabel chiles in hot water until softened, about 15 minutes.

In a large oven-proof stew pot, add the olive oil and onions. Sauté over medium heat until onions are soft and translucent. Reduce heat to low and add garlic, bell peppers, zucchini, yellow squash, tomatoes, chipotle sauce, parsley, red pepper, oregano, and 1/2 teaspoon of kosher salt. Remove chiles from water, seed, chop finely, and add to pot. Increase heat to medium and simmer for 15 minutes, uncovered. Meanwhile, preheat oven to 350°

Turn vegetables gently to mix well, cover, and bake in oven for 30 minutes, or until all vegetables are tender but not soggy.

Serves 8

Cabbage and Apple Slaw with Yogurt Dressing

Hot sauce can dress up many salads—from cole slaw to potato salad to tuna salad.

SLAW

1/2 head each red and green cabbage, shredded
1/4 cup parsley, chopped
1/4 cup cilantro leaves, chopped
1 large apple, peeled, cored, and diced
4 scallions, chopped
1 tablespoon minced gingerroot

YOGURT DRESSING

1 cup yogurt
2 tablespoons honey
1/3 cup orange juice
1 tablespoon Inner Beauty or another habanero
    hot sauce with an aromatic heat
Salt (optional)

Combine ingredients for slaw and mix thoroughly. In a bowl, mix together ingredients for dressing, then add to slaw and toss together. Add salt to taste if desired.

Serves 6

Howlin' Hot Chicken Papaya Coleslaw

You'll never look at coleslaw the same way again! The heat will get you howlin', but the sweet fresh papaya will keep you coming back for more. For variety, fill a hoagie roll with this slaw for an unusual sandwich. For a milder slaw, use 1 tablespoon or less hot sauce.

> 1/4 head each red and green cabbage, finely shredded
> 1/2 bunch cilantro, chopped
> 4 scallions, chopped
> 1 to 2 tablespoons Coyote Cocina Howlin' Hot Sauce
>   or another habanero hot sauce
> Juice of 1 orange
> Juice of 1 lime
> 2 tablespoons sesame oil
> 1/2 pound boneless, skinless chicken breast, cooked
>   and julienned
> 1 ripe papaya, peeled and sliced

In a large bowl, combine cabbage, cilantro, and scallions, and toss. Add hot sauce, orange and lime juices, and sesame oil, and mix thoroughly. Add chicken and toss. Arrange on serving platter or plates, and lay slices of papaya over the top.

Serves 4 to 6

Baked Beans

This dish has a sweet heat—the sweetness of the molasses melds beautifully with the spicy flavors of the hot sauce.

> 1 16-ounce bag dry navy or Great Northern beans
> 2 tablespoons olive oil
> 1 onion, finely chopped
> 1/2 cup dark molasses
> 1/3 cup packed dark brown sugar
> 1/4 cup Devil Drops or another hot habanero sauce
> 1 tablespoon dry mustard
> 2 teaspoons salt
> 1/2 teaspoon coarsely ground black pepper

Rinse beans with cold water and discard any stones. In a
large (5-quart) saucepot or casserole dish with ovenproof
lid, heat beans and 12 cups water to boiling, and cook
5 minutes. Remove from heat, cover, and let stand 1 hour.
Drain and rinse beans.

Preheat oven to 350°. In the same saucepot, over medium-
high heat, heat the olive oil and cook onions until tender.
Stir in beans and 8 cups water. Heat to boiling over high
heat. Cover and bake 1 hour. Stir in the molasses, brown
sugar, hot sauce, dry mustard, salt, and pepper, then cover,
and continue baking another 1 hour, stirring occasionally.
Remove cover, and bake 1 1/2 hours longer, or until beans
are of desired consistency.

Serves 8

Caramelized Onion and Olive Tart

The sweetness of the caramelized onions and olives, combined with the subtle heat of the seeded jalapeños, makes
a wonderful brunch or is terrific as part of a buffet.

CRUST

> 1 1/2 cups all-purpose flour
> 6 tablespoons unsalted butter
> 2 teaspoons fennel seeds, crushed
> 1/2 teaspoon salt
> 3—4 tablespoons cold water

FILLING

> 3 tablespoons olive oil
> 2 large Spanish onions, thinly sliced
> 1/2 cup kalamata olives, pitted and coarsely chopped
> 2 jalapeño chiles, seeded and finely diced
> 3 large eggs
> 1 cup heavy or whipping cream
> 1/2 cup milk
> 1 tablespoon Dijon-style mustard
> 1 tablespoon Cholula Hot Sauce or another hot sauce
> 3/4 teaspoon salt
> 1/2 teaspoon coarsely ground black pepper
> 1/4 teaspoon ground nutmeg
> 1 cup shredded Italian fontina cheese
> 1 tablespoon fresh chopped thyme leaves

To prepare crust, preheat oven to 350°. In a large bowl, combine flour, butter, fennel seeds, and salt until mixture resembles coarse meal. With a fork, stir in the water, working the dough with your fingers until it comes together. Shape the dough into a 6-inch disc, wrap, and refrigerate until chilled, about 30 minutes to 1 hour. On a lightly floured surface, roll dough into a 13-inch round. Place dough into an 11-inch tart pan with removable bottom. Trim edges. Prick dough all over with a fork. Line with aluminum foil and fill with dried beans. Bake 15 to 20 minutes. Remove foil and beans, and bake 15 minutes longer, or until the pastry is slightly golden. Remove to a wire rack to cool.

To prepare the filling, heat the olive oil in a large skillet over medium heat. Add the onions, olives, and jalapeños. Cover and cook until the onions are very soft and tender, about 15 minutes. Remove from the heat and cool. In a large bowl, beat the eggs, heavy cream, milk, mustard, hot sauce, salt, pepper, and nutmeg until blended. Stir in cooled onion mixture. Line bottom of tart shell with shredded cheese. Spoon onion mixture evenly into tart shell. Bake 45 minutes or until set. Remove tart to wire rack to cool. Sprinkle with chopped thyme. Unmold carefully, and serve warm or at room temperature.

Serves 6

Shrimp Wontons with Peanut Dipping Sauce

This is a great appetizer to start any stir-fry or grilled fish entrée. The tangy dipping sauce highlights the simple, fresh flavors in the wontons.

WONTON FILLING

2 tablespoons olive oil
1 tablespoon sesame oil
2 tablespoons minced gingerroot
4 cups chopped bok choy or Chinese cabbage
1/2 pound cooked shrimp, chopped
1 tablespoon Caribbean-style habanero hot sauce
   with a fruity finish
4 scallions, chopped
2 tablespoons rice wine vinegar
1 tablespoon soy sauce

28 wonton wrappers
2 cups chicken stock
1 tablespoon soy sauce
1 tablespoon rice wine vinegar

1 1/2 cups Peanut Dipping Sauce (recipe follows)

Heat both oils in a wok or skillet, and sauté ginger and bok choy over medium-low heat for a few minutes. Cover and cook for 15-20 minutes, or until tender. Add shrimp, hot sauce, scallions, vinegar, and soy sauce, stir, and remove from the heat. Place a heaping teaspoon of mixture in the center of each wonton wrapper, wet the edges with water, and seal with a fork. Combine stock, soy sauce, and rice wine vinegar in a saucepan and bring to a simmer. Cook wontons for 3-4 minutes in the broth, strain with a slotted spoon, and serve immediately. (Any leftover broth—and leftover wontons—can be used for a delicious soup.)

Makes 28 wontons

Peanut Dipping Sauce

    2 tablespoons chopped cilantro
    4 scallions, chopped
    1 tablespoon brown sugar
    1/2 cup crunchy peanut butter
    Juice of 1 lime
    2 teaspoons soy sauce
    1/4 cup chicken stock
    3 tablespoons 911 or another Caribbean
        habanero hot sauce with a fruity finish

To make dipping sauce, combine all ingredients with a
whisk or fork. Set aside while preparing the wontons.

Makes 1 1/2 cups

Tropical Rock Shrimp Ceviche

Ceviche is a simple dish made by "cooking" fish by
marinating it in lime juice. The flavor is light and fresh;
the ripe papaya combines deliciously with the tangy lime
flavor and heat of the salsa. Serve with fried flour tortilla
chips or on your favorite greens.

    1 pound fresh rock shrimp, cleaned and deveined
    1 1/2 cups lime juice, freshly squeezed
    1/2 cup tequila
    1 cup diced fresh papaya
    1/3 cup cilantro leaves, chopped
    2 teaspoons sugar
    1/2 teaspoon salt
    1/4 cup diced tomatoes
    1/3 cup diced jicama, or 1/4 cup diced tomatoes
    1/4 cup chopped scallions
    2 tablespoons Spitfire Red Hot Pepper Sauce
        or another habanero hot sauce
    Lime wedges for garnish

Combine shrimp and lime, mixing well. Refrigerate for
up to 4 hours, stirring frequently, to "cook" the shrimp in
the marinade. Drain marinade from shrimp, and combine
shrimp with remaining ingredients. Garnish with lime.

Serves 4

Rock Shrimp Salad with Spicy Cilantro–Pumpkin Seed Dressing

This dish has a fresh flavor and subtle heat. I've always enjoyed the texture of rock shrimp—almost like lobster—but you can substitute your favorite shrimp.

> 1 pound cleaned and cooked rock shrimp
> 1 cup Spicy Cilantro-Pumpkin Seed Dressing
>   (recipe follows)
> 1/2 pound Bibb lettuce or mixed salad greens
> 1/2 small red onion, finely diced
> 1 red bell pepper, julienned
> 1/4 cup green shelled pumpkin seeds, toasted

Combine shrimp with 1/4 cup dressing. Toss greens with remaining dressing in a salad bowl, and divide salad among plates. Decorate each plate with shrimp, and sprinkle with red onion, bell pepper, and pumpkin seeds.

Serves 6

Spicy Cilantro–Pumpkin Seed Dressing

> 1/2 cup green shelled pumpkin seeds
> 1/3 cup coarsely chopped cilantro
> 1 tablespoon toasted ground coriander
> 1 teaspoon salt
> 2 tomatillos, husked, rinsed, and quartered
> 1 tablespoon Isla Vieques Caribe Fire, or another
>   Caribbean habanero hot sauce
> 1 cup sour cream
> 1 cup buttermilk

In a food processor or blender, combine pumpkin seeds, cilantro, coriander, salt, tomatillos, and hot sauce. Add sour cream and blend. With the machine running, add the buttermilk.

Makes 3 cups

Asian Noodles with Chile Shrimp and Cashews

This dish can be served hot, but if you make it in advance and let it cool to room temperature, you can enjoy it as a spicy main-course salad.

1/2 pound dried Chinese-style noodles or vermicelli
3 tablespoons peanut oil
1 pound large shrimp, shelled and deveined
2 cloves garlic, minced
1 tablespoon grated gingerroot
4 scallions, thinly sliced
1 large red bell pepper, julienned
1 large yellow bell pepper, julienned
2 tablespoons Jump Up and Kiss Me Hot Sauce with Passion
1 tablespoon Chinese chile paste
1 tablespoon light soy sauce
1 tablespoon sesame oil
2 teaspoons honey
1/2 cup toasted cashews

In a large pot of boiling salted water, cook the noodles, breaking up with a fork, until tender, about 3 minutes. Drain well and toss with 1 tablespoon of the oil. In a large skillet over medium-high heat, heat 1 tablespoon oil and cook the shrimp until they turn pink, about 3 minutes. Transfer to plate. In same skillet over medium-high heat, heat remaining tablespoon oil and cook garlic and ginger until fragrant, about 1 minute. Stir in scallions and bell peppers. Cook until tender, about 3 minutes. In a small bowl, combine the hot sauce, chile paste, soy sauce, sesame oil, and honey until blended. Stir into skillet with the vegetables. Stir in shrimp and cashews, and heat to boiling. Remove from heat. In a large bowl, toss noodles with vegetables and shrimp. Serve immediately.

Serves 6

Pan-Fried Scallops with Chiles, Tomatoes, and Tequila

Serve these scallops with warmed flour tortillas or a loaf of hearty bread, or anything that will allow you to soak up the sauce. It's also good served with Green Tabasco Rice (page 136) or over pasta.

- 2 tablespoons olive oil
- 2 cloves garlic, minced
- 1 1/2 pounds sea scallops, sliced widthwise
- 4 plum or regular tomatoes, diced small
- 6 scallions, chopped
- 2 fresh serrano or jalapeño chiles, finely chopped
- 1/2 cup tequila
- 2 tablespoons Tapatio, Salsa Huichol, or another red chile hot sauce
- 1 teaspoon salt
- Juice of 1 lime plus lime wedges for garnish
- 1/4 cup butter, at room temperature

In a large skillet, heat oil. Add garlic and sauté for 1 minute, stirring, until lightly browned. Add sea scallops and sauté on medium-high heat for 4 minutes, or until browned on both sides. Add tomatoes, scallions, and chiles, and stir to combine. Add tequila carefully, since it may flame up as you add it. Bring it to a boil and allow to reduce slightly. (The scallops create their own juices.) Add hot sauce, salt, and lime juice and stir. Lower heat to just above simmer and stir in the butter, moving the pan the entire time. When butter is incorporated into the sauce, remove from heat and serve immediately. Garnish with lime wedges.

Serves 6

Indonesian Coconut-Almond Shrimp

The flavors in this dish are subtle, yet complex. Serve with
a simple side dish of rice with raisins, various chutneys,
and fresh papaya or mango. Cabbage and Apple Slaw with
Yogurt Dressing (page 125) is also a nice accompaniment.

> 3 tablespoons Sambal Wayang Bawang Putih
>   (Indonesian Sambal Sauce) or another sweet,
>   savory, hot sauce with a thick and rich texture
> 1 tablespoon Windmill Red Hot Sauce or other
>   habanero sauce with onion and a little vinegar
> 1/2 teaspoon salt
> Juice of 1 orange
> Juice of 1 lime
> 1 pound medium shrimp, peeled, deveined,
>   and tails removed
> 1 cup shredded, sweetened coconut
> 1 cup sliced almonds
> 1 small bunch cilantro leaves
> 1/4 teaspoon salt

Mix together hot sauces, salt, and orange and lime juices,
and toss with shrimp. Set aside to marinate for 1 hour. In
a food processor, combine coconut, almonds, cilantro, and
salt. Preheat oven to broil. Heat a large sauté pan and add the
shrimp and marinating juices. Sauté quickly until shrimp turn
opaque, about 6 minutes. Remove from heat and arrange in
baking dish in one layer. Top with coconut-almond mixture
to cover and place under broiler. (Do not put too close to
heat or leave under broiler for long, as the coconut and
almonds will burn easily.) Lightly brown and heat through.

Serves 4

Chicken Salad with Tomato and Avocado

This spicy, cool chicken salad is refreshing on a hot summer day. Flour tortillas are cut into thin strips and fried, then sprinkled on top for added flavor and crunch.

> 4 skinless, boneless chicken breast halves
>   (about 1 1/4 pounds)
> 1/4 cup peanut oil
> 2 10-inch flour tortillas, cut into 1/4-inch strips
> 3 tablespoons olive oil
> 1 tablespoon grated lemon zest
> 2 tablespoons lemon juice
> 1 tablespoon or more Trinidad Extra Hot Habanero
>   Pepper Sauce or another habanero hot sauce
> 1 clove garlic, minced
> 3/4 teaspoon salt
> 1/2 teaspoon coarsely ground black pepper
> 3 scallions, thinly sliced
> 1/4 cup finely chopped cilantro
> 1 large tomato, cut into 1/2-inch chunks
> 1 large avocado, peeled, seeded, and cut into
>   1/2-inch chunks

In a large saucepan, place the chicken breasts in 4 cups cold water. Bring to a boil, cover, and cook over medium heat for 6–8 minutes. Transfer chicken to a plate, and set aside.

In a skillet over medium-high heat, heat the peanut oil until very hot. Cook tortilla strips in small batches until lightly browned. With a slotted spoon, remove to paper towels to drain. In a large bowl, whisk together olive oil, lemon zest, lemon juice, hot sauce, garlic, salt, pepper, scallions, and cilantro. Cut chicken breasts lengthwise into thin strips. Add to bowl with dressing. Gently stir in tomato and avocado. Divide chicken mixture evenly onto plates and top with tortilla strips.

Serves 4

Roasted Chile Rubbed Chicken

This dish is delicious with Green Tabasco Rice (recipe follows), or Salsa Mexicana (page 138). If you have leftovers, remove the chicken from the bone and use as a filling for burritos or tacos.

MARINADE

2 tablespoons ground cumin
2 tablespoons ground coriander
8 cloves garlic, minced
1/2 teaspoon salt
1/4 cup olive oil
1/4 cup Salsa Huichol, La Guaca-Maya, or any hot sauce made with dried red chiles and with a rich finish

1 1/2 pounds chicken (thighs, legs, whole chicken, or any combination)

Combine marinade ingredients, coat chicken all over with this mixture, and let sit for 4 hours or overnight. Preheat oven to 375° and bake chicken for approximately 40 minutes, depending on which cuts you use.

Serves 4

Green Tabasco Rice

You'll never return to plain rice after sampling this rice, which goes well with chicken or ribs. Use green Tabasco, or your favorite hot sauce. (If you use a habanero hot sauce, you should lessen the amount.)

2 cups rice
4 tablespoons Tabasco Jalapeño Sauce or another hot sauce
6 scallions, chopped
3 tablespoons fresh chopped cilantro
2 tablespoons fresh chopped parsley

Bring 4 cups of water to boil in a pot, add rice, reduce heat, and allow to simmer, covered, for 15 minutes. Stir in hot sauce, and simmer for 5 more minutes. When rice is done, remove from heat, sprinkle with scallions, cilantro, and parsley, and serve.

Serves 4

Jump Up and Kiss My Whole Roasted Chicken

Garlic and chiles are two of the oldest aphrodisiacs known to man. Guests will want to kiss the chef after one bite—if not before—when they catch the lovely aromas wafting from the kitchen.

> 1/4 cup Jump Up and Kiss Me Hot Sauce with Passion or another papaya-based habanero hot sauce
> Juice of 1 lemon
> Juice of 1 lime
> Juice of 1 orange
> 1 teaspoon salt
> 5 cloves garlic, sliced
> 1 whole chicken (about 4 pounds)
> 4 carrots
> 1 large yellow onion
> 2 baking potatoes
> Freshly ground pepper

Combine hot sauce, juices, and salt. With a small sharp knife, make little slits all over the chicken, and slide the garlic slices into the slits. Put any remaining garlic into cavity. Pour marinade over chicken, adding some to the cavity, and let sit, basting frequently, for 1 hour. (Or put in a plastic bag and turn frequently.) Preheat oven to 350°. Cut carrots, onion, and potatoes into large chunks, and put into a baking dish with the chicken. Grind pepper over all. Bake for 3/4 hour, turning vegetables and basting chicken occasionally, then lower heat to 325° and cook for another 3/4 hour, or until chicken and vegetables are cooked through.

Serves 4 to 6

Crab and Avocado Tacos with Salsa Mexicana

These tacos are easy to serve and have a wonderfully fresh flavor.

SALSA MEXICANA

- 1 large ripe tomato, diced
- 1/2 small red onion, finely diced
- 2 tablespoons chopped cilantro
- 1 serrano chile, finely chopped
- Juice of 1 lime
- 2 tablespoons Pico Pica or another smooth, tangy, red chile hot sauce

GREEN TABASCO SOUR CREAM

- 1 cup sour cream
- 1/4 cup Tabasco Jalapeño Sauce
- 4 scallions, chopped

- 1 pound fresh Dungeness crabmeat or imitation crabmeat
- 2 ripe Haas avocados
- 1 lemon
- 2 tablespoons vegetable oil
- 10 corn tortillas
- 3 cups finely shredded green cabbage

Combine Salsa Mexicana ingredients in a small bowl, toss, and set aside. In a separate bowl, combine sour cream with Tabasco and scallions. Toss with crabmeat. Slice avocados on a plate and squeeze lemon juice over slices. In a skillet, heat vegetable oil over medium-low heat and cook each tortilla briefly on both sides until soft, not crisp. Drain on paper towels. To arrange tacos, lay tortillas flat on each serving plate and place about 2 tablespoons crab mix on one side. Top with a few avocado slices, then with the shredded cabbage. Fold in half and spoon the Salsa Mexicana over the top of each taco.

Makes 10 tacos

Spicy Black Bean Tortillas with Chipotle Cream Sauce

These tortillas are simple and easy to prepare. They are a great accompaniment to any main dish, or to make a meal of them, jazz them up by serving with guacamole, different fresh salsas, and fried potatoes.

> 1 tablespoon vegetable oil
> 1 yellow or white onion, diced
> 1 green bell pepper, diced
> 1 tablespoon ground cumin
> 3 tablespoons Tamazula Salsa Picante or
>   another smooth, rich red chile sauce
> 4 cups cooked black beans
> Salt
> 1 cup sour cream
> 1 1/2 tablespoons chipotle hot sauce
> 16 flour tortillas, wrapped in foil and warmed in
>   a 350° oven for 10 minutes
> Shredded lettuce for garnish
> Chopped tomatoes for garnish
> Queso Cotija or any Mexican cheese that can
>   be crumbled for garnish
> Sliced avocados for garnish

Heat oil in a saucepan and sauté onion and pepper until soft. Add cumin, hot sauce, beans, and salt to taste and cook until beans are heated. In a small bowl, mix sour cream and chipotle sauce. Holding a tortilla in the palm of your hand, spoon a line of chipotle sour cream down the center of the tortilla, and add the bean mixture. Top with lettuce, tomatoes, cheese, and avocados, roll up, and serve.

Serves 8

Chipotle Rubbed Pork Loin

The smoky heat of the chipotle chiles combined with honey is a lovely accent to the pork, which is delicious roasted or grilled. Serve this dish with Spicy Black Bean Tortillas with Chipotle Cream Sauce (page 139). If you have leftovers, make an orange-jicama roasted pork salad.

> **4 cloves garlic, minced**
> **Juice of 1 lemon**
> **1/4 cup honey**
> **1/4 cup chipotle hot sauce**
> **2 ancho chiles, reconstituted and finely chopped**
> **1 teaspoon salt**
> **1 tablespoon chile powder**
> **1 1/2 pounds pork tenderloin**
> **Orange slices for garnish**

Combine garlic, lemon juice, honey, hot sauce, chiles, salt, and chile powder. Rub all over pork loin, refrigerate, and marinate for 4 hours or overnight. Bring pork to room temperature just before cooking. Preheat oven to 350°. In a roasting pan, roast pork for approximately 40 minutes, basting occasionally, or until a thermometer inserted into center of pork registers 160°. (If the marinade gets dry, cover roast for last 15 minutes. Or, for a crispy crust, add a little warm water to the pan and place under the broiler for the last 8 minutes of cooking.) Remove from the oven and let sit for 10 minutes before carving. Serve with fresh orange slices.

Serves 4

Barbecue Pork Ribs

If you live in a place where the weather is fickle, indoor barbecue is the way to go. Whether from your oven or from the grill, these tender ribs must be served with bread instead of napkins so you don't miss a drop of this sweet, tangy barbecue sauce.

MARINADE

> **1/2 cup finely diced yellow onion**
> **1/3 cup dark molasses**
> **1/3 cup honey**
> **1 cup ketchup**
> **4 cloves garlic, minced**

2 tablespoons Walker's Wood Jerk Seasoning or
   another spicy jerk sauce
2 tablespoons Dijon-style mustard

3 pounds country-style pork ribs

Combine marinade ingredients, mix well, and pour over ribs. Marinate for 4 hours. Preheat oven to 350°. Cover ribs and cook for 1/2 hour. Remove cover, lower temperature to 325°, and cook for an additional 20-30 minutes. (Or, remove from oven after initial 1/2 hour and finish on the grill.)

Serves 4

Smoky Chipotle Grilled Tuna Niçoise

1/2 cup Montezuma Smoky Chipotle Hot Sauce
   or another chipotle sauce
Juice of 1 lime
Juice of 1 orange
2 tablespoons olive oil
4 5-ounce pieces of tuna
1/2 pound assorted greens
4 medium red potatoes, cooked and sliced in
   1/4-inch rounds
1/2 pound green beans, blanched
Oil-cured olives for garnish
Chipotle-Citrus Dressing (recipe follows)
Lime wedges for garnish

Whisk together hot sauce, lime and orange juices, and olive oil, and pour over tuna, making sure to coat all surfaces. Marinate for 2 hours. Prepare grill (or turn oven to broil). Place tuna on grill and mark twice on each side by cooking 3–4 minutes, then rotating the tuna 1/4 inch in another direction to create grill marks. Repeat on other side. (Or, broil for 4 minutes on each side to sear outer flesh.) Remove tuna from heat. (Note: Tuna will be rare inside. If you prefer, grill or broil for another 4 minutes.) To serve, arrange greens on each plate, top with tuna, and arrange sliced potatoes, green beans, and olives around tuna. Serve with Chipotle-Citrus Dressing and fresh lime wedges.

Serves 4

Chipotle-Citrus Dressing

Don't limit this dressing to tuna; serve it drizzled over fresh tomatoes, asparagus, even rice.

> 1 1/2 cups extra virgin olive oil
> 2 tablespoons finely chopped red onion
> 2 tablespoons chipotle hot sauce
> 1 tablespoon Dijon-style mustard
> 2 tablespoons lime juice, freshly squeezed
> 2 tablespoons orange juice, freshly squeezed
> Salt and freshly ground black pepper to taste

Blend together the oil, onion, and hot sauce in a blender or food processor. Whisk in the remaining ingredients.

Makes 1 2/3 cups

Christmas Huevos Rancheros

Eggs can be easily turned into a special breakfast or brunch dish. Despite the name (which comes from the red and green salsas), these huevos can be eaten any time of the year—holiday or not!

> 2 cups cooked black beans, seasoned with 1 minced
>   jalapeño, 1 minced clove garlic, 1 tablespoon
>   ground coriander, and salt to taste
> 2 tablespoons chopped cilantro
> 6 scallions, chopped
> 1 ripe avocado, diced
> 1/8 to 1/4 cup El Yucateco green hot sauce or
>   another fiery green hot sauce
> Vegetable oil
> 8 corn tortillas
> 8 large eggs
> 2 cups shredded jack and/or Cheddar cheese
> 1 1/2 cups Salsa Mexicana (see page 138)
> Cilantro sprigs for garnish

Preheat broiler. Have beans hot and ready to serve. Combine cilantro, scallions, avocado, and hot sauce to make the green salsa. Set aside. In a large skillet, heat 1-2 tablespoons vegetable oil (just enough to coat the pan). Heat each tortilla briefly on both sides in hot oil, just long enough to soften and heat through. Remove and drain on paper towels. Fry the eggs, sunny side up or as you like them. While the eggs are cooking, arrange 2 corn tortillas, side by side, on each ovenproof serving plate. Place some beans on each tortilla, place cheese on top of beans, and melt cheese under broiler. Top each tortilla with an egg. Put some green salsa on top of one egg, and Salsa Mexicana on top of the other egg. Garnish with cilantro sprigs.

Serves 4

Green Eggs and Red Ham

Dr. Seuss would be proud. If your kids like a bit of heat with their breakfast, but nothing too hot, they'll love this. Otherwise save it for a cozy breakfast on a rainy day or for a Sunday brunch. Serve with bagels or hearty breakfast rolls.

> **8 large eggs**
> **1/3 cup milk**
> **1/2 teaspoon salt**
> **Freshly ground black pepper**
> **1 tablespoon Chef Hans' Jalapeño Hot Sauce**
>   **or another green hot sauce**
> **3 tablespoons chopped parsley**
> **4 scallions, chopped**
> **4 tablespoons maple syrup**
> **2 tablespoons Panola Cajun Hot Sauce or another**
>   **with deep red color and tangy, red pepper heat**
> **4 slices ham, 1/4 inch thick**
> **2 tablespoons butter**

Whisk together eggs, milk, salt, and black pepper. Add green hot sauce, parsley, and scallions, and set aside. Preheat broiler. Combine maple syrup and hot sauce and pour over ham. In a large skillet, heat butter until melted, then add egg mixture. While eggs are cooking, place ham under broiler. Scramble the eggs. Turn ham once so it colors nicely on both sides. To serve, spoon some of the ham liquid on each plate, and top with ham and then some eggs. (You can also emphasize the green and red by adding mixed finely diced tomatoes and red peppers onto the ham and chopped fresh herbs into the eggs.)

Serves 4

Sources

Hot Sauce Shops

(most of which also mail-order)

Calido Chile Traders
Oak Park Mall
Oak Park, KS 66214
800-LOTT-HOT
More than thirty other locations.

Caribbean Spice Company
2 South Church Street
Fairhope, AL 36532
800-990-6088

Coyote General Store
132 West Water Street
Santa Fe, NM 87501
800-866-HOWL

Hot, Hot, Hot
56 South Delacey Avenue
Pasadena, CA 91105
800-959-7742

Hot Salsas
Seaport Village
San Diego, CA 92101

Le Saucier
Faneuil Hall Marketplace
Boston, MA 02109
617-227-9649

Old Santa Fe Pottery
2485 South Santa Fe Drive
Denver, CO 80223
303-871-9434

Peppers
2009 Highway One
Dewey Beach, DE 19971
800-998-FIRE

Some Like It Hot
3208 Scott Street
San Francisco, CA 94123
415-441-7468

Supernatural Food
142 Walton Street
Syracuse, NY 13202
315-424-2545

Mail-Order Sources

Chile Head
23 Banks Street
Somerville, MA 02144
800-4WE-BURN

Flamingo Flats
P.O. Box 441
St. Michael's, MD 21663
800-468-8841

Hot and Spicy Foods Company
P.O. Box 1986
Morgan Hill, CA 95038
800-64-SPICY

Hot Sauce Harry's
3422 Flair Drive
Dallas, TX 75229
800-588-8979

Hot Stuff
P.O. Box 2210, Stuyvesant Station
New York, NY 10009
800-WANT-HOT
hotstuffny@aol.com

International Hot Stuff
905 North California Street
Chicago, IL 60622
800-555-9798

Island Hoppers
P.O. Box 37
St. John, U.S. Virgin Islands 00831
809-693-7200

Mo Hotta Mo Betta
P.O. Box 4136
San Luis Obispo, CA 93403
800-462-3220

Salsas, Etc.
126 Great Mall Way
Milpitas, CA 95035
800-40-SALSA

Hot Sauce of the Month Clubs

Chile Today Hot Tamale
Hot Sauce of the Month Club
919 Highway 33, #47
Freehold, NJ 07728
800-468-7377

Hot Sauce Club of America
P.O. Box 687
Indian Rocks Beach,
FL 34635-0687
800-SAUCE-2U

Red Hots Pepper Sauce of the Month Club
P.O. Box 31
Indian Rocks Beach, FL 34635
800-973-3468

Hot Sauce Collectors

Andrew Keeler
5798 Honors Drive
San Diego, CA 92122
akeeler@aol.com
Keeler is putting together an informal exchange of information with other collectors.

Chip Hearn
Starboard Restaurant
2009 Highway 1
Dewey Beach, DE 19971
800-998-FIRE
Chip also owns Peppers (previous page).

Also by Jennifer Trainer Thompson

Trail of Flame
An irreverent guide to spicy restaurants and the culture of hot, listing many of the restaurants whose sauces are featured here.
$11.95 paperback, 192 pages

Hot Sauce Posters
A beautiful set of posters highlighting 249 hot sauces in screaming color. A great guide to starting a hot sauce collection! $15.00 each, or both for $25.00

Ten Speed Press, P.O. Box 7123,
Berkeley, California 94707
(800) 841-2665

For more information about
books, posters, sauces, and products by Jennifer Trainer Thompson,
contact JT[2] Productions, 560 North Hoosac Road,
Williamstown, MA 01267

or E-mail Jennifer at 75050.1417@compuserve.com

Index